LE 6 MACLE

ISECT 14 EARTH-

SLATER 30 GIANT

TID 38 MILLIPEDE

54 AUSTRALIAN

LINDERS RANGES

L ANT 78 FRESH-

RASPY CRICKET

EROR GUM MOTH

LEAF INSECT 120

CHRIS HUMFREY'S
COOLEST CREEPY CRAWLIES

To view the videos
scan the QR codes
with your phone
or go to
newhollandpublishers.com/coolest
and enter the
unique codes

CHRIS HUMFREY'S
COOLEST
CREEPY
CRAWLIES

**Delve into the fascinating micro world of
Australia's incredible invertebrate creatures**

Photographs by Jay Town

CONTENTS

Introduction

Welcome into my *wild* world of creepy crawlies! My earliest childhood memories are of being surrounded by animals. I have always marvelled at the extraordinary beauty of creatures, and the amazing jobs every species plays in maintaining healthy ecosystems.

Luckily for me, I grew up with a very supportive mum and dad who helped nurture my wonderment for nature. When I was a kid I had a veritable zoo in my very own backyard. From a young age I was heavily involved in my local Field Naturalists group, allowing me access to fabulous wildlife experts and mentors.

My thirst for learning led me to study a Bachelor of Science at the University of Melbourne majoring in Zoology and Botany. I now own my very own wildlife facility in the picturesque Macedon Ranges of Victoria, which is home to a myriad of diverse Australian wildlife.

My home country Australia is crammed full of totally awesome, unique and sometimes scary creatures. However, it's the miniature world of invertebrates which I find utterly fascinating. When you look a little more closely, the ordinary becomes extraordinary and breathtakingly beautiful.

In this book, I hope to share my knowledge of Australian invertebrates with you. I firmly believe that if you understand a little bit more about a certain species, you'll develop a greater appreciation for it, and will be more likely to save it, instead of *'squishing it!'*

Our planet has never faced so many environmental challenges. We all need to do our part in making the world a better place. Just like your mum and dad, every species has a job to do too, an ecological niche. Remember, we can't just save our favourites – we also must save and protect the scary, bizarre, 'not so attractive', and sometimes the downright dangerous creatures too!

In a healthy world, all animals are interconnected and vital for harmony and balance. The protection of biodiversity also creates a healthier and happier environment for people. Education and knowledge are the key to conservation.

I hope that you spend many wonderful and engaging hours reading and re-reading my *Coolest Creepy Crawlies* book. Enjoy my video clips too! And let's look after the planet together.

Chris Humfrey,
Zoologist

Rhinoceros Beetle

Xylotrupes ulysses

'Meet the sumo wrestler of the bug world!'

Beetles have lived on our planet for over 300 million years! Amazingly there are more species of beetles on Earth than any other animal. One unique and exceedingly strong species is found right here in Australia, and it's called the rhinoceros beetle.

WOW, that's like a person lifting a double-decker bus over their head!

For its size the rhinoceros beetle is one of the strongest creatures in the world. It can lift 850 times its own body weight.

Classification

KINGDOM:	Animalia
PHYLUM:	Arthropoda
CLASS:	Insecta
ORDER:	Coleoptera
FAMILY:	Scarabaeidae
GENUS:	*Xylotrupes*
SPECIES:	*ulysses*

What's in a name?

Affectionately called **'rhino' beetles** because they superficially resemble a horned pachyderm, the rhinoceros. Beetles belong to the order Coleoptera. In Latin this translates to 'insect with sheathed wings' – *koleos* meaning 'sheathed', *pteron* meaning 'winged'. This arrangement ensures that the hard **elytra** protect the soft hind wings.

As rhinoceros beetles are insects they have an **exoskeleton** made from **chitin** (protein). Their bodies are hollow and dry, with no blood or muscle.

It is in fact Australia's largest beetle, and is one of my favourite insects. It reminds me of Darth Vader from *Star Wars*.

Where is it found?

Beetles can be found all over Australia, but if you're looking for this species of rhinoceros beetle in the southern states you'll be out of luck! This rhino beetle prefers warm and humid environments along the coasts of northern New South Wales, Queensland and the Northern Territory. However, Australia is home to over **200 different species** of rhino beetle – oddly enough most of them don't have horns!

Beetles occur in many varied and different habitats, including in soil, flowers, fruit or leaf litter, under rocks or tree bark, or digging their way into the tree. Their favourite place to hang out is in introduced **poinciana trees**. They often congregate in huge numbers, feasting on the succulent juicy new foliage. These large congregations of males and females create a reproductive frenzy. Rhino Beetles are most commonly found in the tree canopy. Their favourite foods are nectar, sap and fruit.

Poinciana trees – introduced from Madagascar – make an excellent food plant for rhino beetles.

Did you know that an animal which favours primarily fruit for their diet is called a FRUGIVORE?

Amazing morphology and adaptations

These insects have six segmented legs, two antennae, compound eyes (a large eye composed of many eye-like structures), and three body parts: the head, thorax and abdomen. They have specially adapted mouth parts. They also have a special covering to protect their wings called the **elytra**. This is what they rub on their abdomen to make a loud scary hissing sound.

It is only the male which 'sports' the prominent forked horns on the front of his body, which protrude from the head and the thorax. The female doesn't have horns whatsoever. The male uses his horns for combat – to ward off potential competitor males by pushing them from the safety of a tree branch.

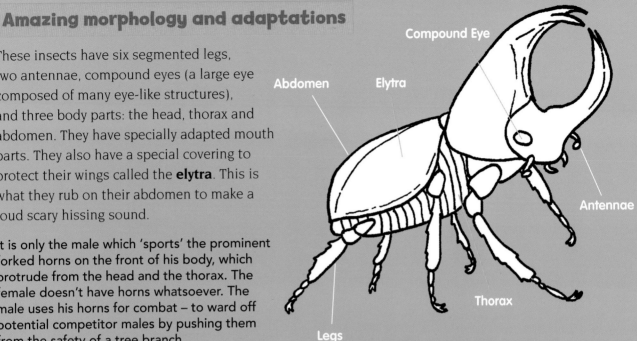

Those horns look like they could make a great can opener.

Rhino beetles have many amazing adaptations to help them to survive. The hard **exoskeleton** protects them from predators and when falling from height. The **elytra** are the first pair of wings that have hardened into a covering, protecting the hind wings and enabling the beetle to live underground. The **horns** are used to pierce fruit to eat, and to fight with other males for a girlfriend.

The **spiky legs** are used to help them dig into the soil and push away dirt or leaf litter. At the end of their legs, they have **hooks** to help them grip on tight wherever they are, and to ensure they don't get thrown out of a tree by another male.

Both males and females can fly strongly and are often attracted to lights around people's homes at night. They will also congregate around streetlights, often in huge numbers.

You would think twice about eating a stinky rhino beetle – you would have to put a peg on your nose.

The hooks remind me of the grappling hooks or ice picks that mountain climbers use!

From personal experience, when picked up, they often exude a foul-smelling odour from their abdomen.

Life Cycle

Rhinoceros beetles are **holometabolous**. That's a fancy way of saying that beetles have four life stages: egg, larva, pupa and adult.

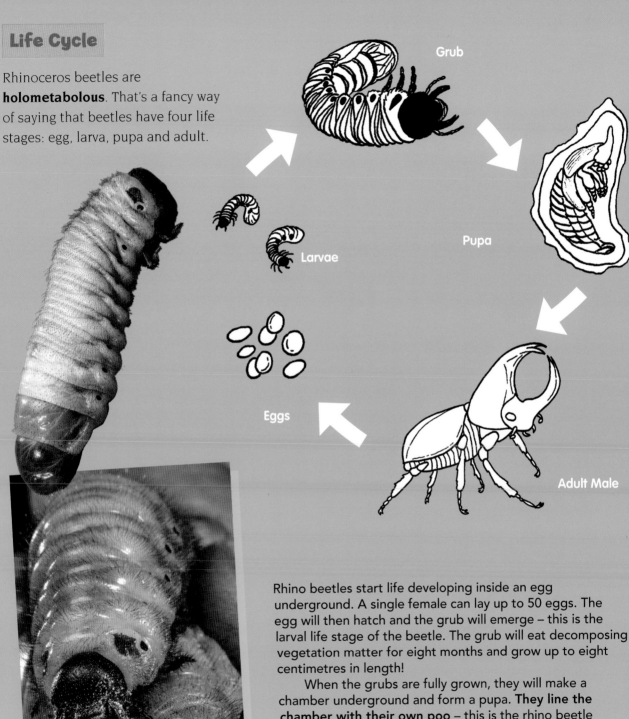

Grub

Larvae

Pupa

Eggs

Adult Male

Rhino beetles start life developing inside an egg underground. A single female can lay up to 50 eggs. The egg will then hatch and the grub will emerge – this is the larval life stage of the beetle. The grub will eat decomposing vegetation matter for eight months and grow up to eight centimetres in length!

When the grubs are fully grown, they will make a chamber underground and form a pupa. **They line the chamber with their own poo** – this is the rhino beetle equivalent to a caterpillar forming a chrysalis! The adult rhino beetle will then crawl out of the pupa and live for around two to four months. The adults will find a mate and lay eggs to continue the life cycle.

Although the female rhino beetle does not 'sport' the fancy horn like the male, she does emit an intoxicating pheromone which drives the boy rhino beetles **CRAZY!**

In fact, rival male rhino beetles compete for the females so intensely that they commonly grapple each other and throw their competitor out of the tree canopy.

Predators

Rhino beetles are eaten by a wide variety of animals. However, they have a very sneaky adaptation of hissing and 'wheezing' in an attempt to scare off would-be predators. They make this alarming noise by rubbing their elytra against their abdomen.

A rhino beetle makes a decent meal for a Laughing Kookaburra.

What's their job?

Rhinoceros beetles are highly important **pollinators** of many Australian plant species. Their larval stage is a very useful **detritivore**, breaking down organic waste in our ecosystems, returning nutrients back into the soil. Rhino beetles are important in the food web as many animals rely on them as a food source.

SCAN HERE
to watch a WILD clip

jthtvf

What can we do to help rhino beetles?

- Create compost and habitat for rhino beetles and other native insects in your back yard.
- Plant a poinciana tree.
- Do not use herbicides and pesticides.

Macleay's Spectre Stick Insect

Extatosoma tiaratum

What's in a name?

'Looks like an alien from another planet.'

Also known as the Giant Prickly Stick Insect, these impressive insects belong to the **phasmid** family. The species was named the 'Macleay's Spectre' after the prominent 19th-century naturalist William Sharp Macleay. The word phasmid (pronounced *fas-mid*) in Greek means spectre or ghost. They certainly are masters of disguise!

That certainly makes a lot of sense, they can definitely blend in with their environment. Now you see me… now you don't.

Did you know that phasmids are related to other groups of insects including mantids, grasshoppers, crickets, katydids and cockroaches? **Extato** comes from the Latin word meaning 'to be outside oneself' and **soma** means 'body'.

Gum trees.

Classification

KINGDOM:	Animalia
PHYLUM:	Arthropoda
CLASS:	Insecta
ORDER:	Phasmatodea
FAMILY:	Phasmatidae
GENUS:	Extatosoma
SPECIES:	tiaratum

Where is it found?

These insects can be found along the warm and humid coasts of northern New South Wales and Queensland. They are **arboreal**, preferring to live in the canopy of a tree or shrub. Being masters of disguise, they expertly blend in with their surroundings. They are one of the most kept pet insects in the world.

Amazing morphology and adaptations

These stick insects are **folivores**, which means that they eat leaves. They particularly love devouring eucalyptus and acacia leaves and are also known to eat rose leaves and blackberry leaves. Unlike their cousin the carnivorous praying mantid.

Looking more like aliens from another planet, you would be excused for thinking that Macleay's Spectre Stick Insects are dangerous, but in fact they can neither bite nor sting.

As they are harmless they must employ some 'crafty' adaptations to ward of potential predators. The most obvious is their incredibly **cryptic camouflage** – their entire body is shaped like a dead old gum leaf. They masterfully sway with the wind and blend into the canopy.
However, if roughly handled, the spikes on their legs can make things a little uncomfortable.

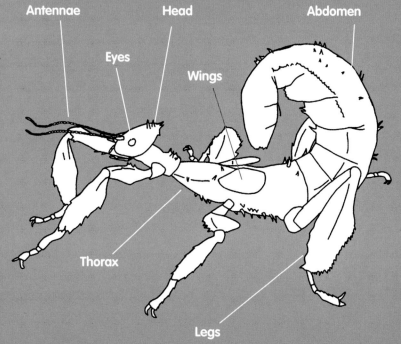

Antennae

Head

Abdomen

Eyes

Wings

Thorax

Legs

These stick insects are also excellent **mimics**, pretending to look like a scorpion by curling up their abdomen to resemble a huge 'stinger'.

Hey, interesting fact...
Did you know that stick insect poo is called FRASS? Now that's a cool new word next time you play Scrabble.

You'd think twice about eating this insect if you were a hungry bird or lizard.

Even their legs look like chewed on gum leaves... that's amazing!

They also raise their front two legs, adopting the attack pose of their cousin the praying mantid!

They use their long antennae to sense and feel around their environment. Unlike you and I these stick insects breathe through their thoracic and abdominal spiracles rather than through their mouth or nose.

WOW, did you know that this stick insect has the ability to grow back their legs again? I wish we could do that.

That is so cool – a bottom-breathing bug!

As they grow bigger, they must shed their exoskeleton. This process is called **ecdysis** or **moulting**. Male spiny leaf insects shed their skin five times before they reach maturity, and females six times.

Life Cycle

You could be forgiven for thinking that the male and female belong to completely different species. The adult female has **vestigial** or **remnant wings** and cannot fly. The male has long lacy wings and is an exceptionally strong flyer.

Eggs

Nymph

> The male reminds me of a wasp with a big stinger, and the female looks like a scorpion with a curled-up tail.

There are positives to being a female Macleay's Spectre Stick Insect. Males are relatively short lived at six months, whereas females generally live up to two years.

These insects have an amazing life cycle! The female can lay thousands of eggs in her lifetime.

Juvenile

> Whoa... that's a lot of hungry mouths to feed!

Macleay's Spectre Stick Insects are **hemimetabolous**. Put simply this means that they have three stages of development: egg, nymph and adult. They do not undergo a complete metamorphosis – the newly hatched nymph (baby) already resembles the adult.

Cleverly, the female flicks each egg out of her egg tube high up in the tree canopy and it lands way below on the forest floor.

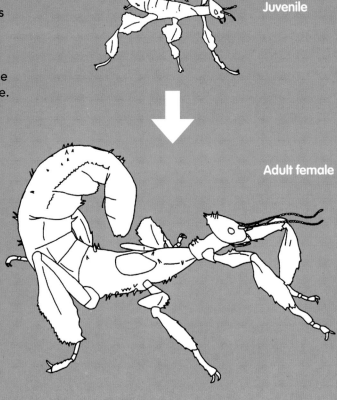

Adult female

The eggs are wonderfully camouflaged, resembling an acacia seed. The egg ingeniously has a little knob on it, called a **capitulum**, that attracts ants.

The ants will take the stick insect egg down into their nest chamber, where they eat the capitulum and the leave the egg alone.

The ant nest is humid and warm and is a perfect environment for the baby stick insect to develop and hatch.

Amazingly, upon hatching the **nymph looks exactly like an ant**. They hastily make their way out of the ant nest, and quickly climb high into the tree canopy. Their 'jerky' ant-like movement and appearance deters predators from snacking on them. After settling in the tree canopy, they start feasting on the newest most succulent leaves. The nymph gradually loses the red/black ant appearance and adopts the colouration of its leafy habitat. The nymphs will grow and shed their exoskeleton, with each instar progressively looking more like the form of an adult.

The most incredible life-cycle fact of this amazing bug is that the female can lay eggs without having to mate with a male. This is called **parthenogenesis**. The female can clone herself! Only females hatch with this reproductive method, and they can take much longer to develop and hatch… sometimes up to three years.

When a male and female Macleay's Spectre Stick Insects mate, the incubation time of the eggs is shortened and both males and females hatch.

The eggs can take anywhere from six months to three years to hatch.

WOWSERS… that's a long time to spend locked up in your bedroom.

Black-faced Cuckooshrikes forage in the canopy for bugs such as stick insects.

Predators

Despite some incredible adaptations to help them survive, these stick insects have plenty of predators. They are often eaten by many different species of lizards, mammals and birds.

What can we do to help phasmids?

- It doesn't matter where you live in Australia or anywhere else in the world, phasmids are found everywhere except Antarctica. The chances are that you will have them living in your local area. Why not plant some habitat and create a food source, so a phasmid can call your home its home too?
- Remember to avoid using pesticides and herbicides in your back yard and be a responsible pet owner. That's correct – a pet cat will easily devour a helpless stick insect.

SCAN HERE
to watch a WILD clip

vimirm

Earthworm

'A most wonderful ecological engineer that can regrow body parts.'

Earthworms have been around for over 600 million years. There are over 2,700 different species worldwide, with some as small as one millimetre and others reaching up to two metres. Australia is home to a giant earthworm native to Victoria, known as the Giant Gippsland Earthworm! "It's only found in a small location and is vulnerable to extinction!"

Talk about concentrated housing – healthy, fertile soil can have around 430 earthworms per square metre.

Classification

KINGDOM: Animalia
PHYLUM: Annelida
CLASS: Clitellata
SUBCLASS: Oligochaeta
ORDER: Opisthopora

What's in a name?

Earthworms belong to the phylum Annelida. The Latin word **anellus** means 'little ring', referring to the earthworm's segmented body.

Unlike their close cousins the bristleworms (Polychaetes), earthworms belong to the subclass known as **Oligochaeta**, which simply translates in Latin as *oligo* meaning 'few' and *khaite* meaning 'long hair', so 'few long hairs'. Earthworms have fewer bristles on their bodies compared to polychaetes.

When I was a kid, I didn't pay a lot of thought to the importance of earthworms, but now I realise that they are so important in our ecosystems, and you'll be amazed how incredible they really are!

Where are they found?

Australian native earthworms can be found in forests all over the country, but they prefer native vegetation and moist habitats. The earthworms in our backyards are mostly an introduced species from Europe. Regardless of their heritage, earthworms are a vital and welcome friend to our environment.

Earthworms play a vital role in maintaining healthy topsoil.

Earthworms are invertebrates and lack a backbone. They are also without a head, eyes, ears or limbs.

Positioned on the front segment of the earthworm, just above the mouth, is the 'beak-like' **prostomium** which closes the mouth while the worm is at rest but can also sense chemicals in the environment.

Amazing morphology and adaptations

Earthworms live most of their lives underground so they have some nifty adaptations to help them survive and thrive in their subterranean world of darkness.

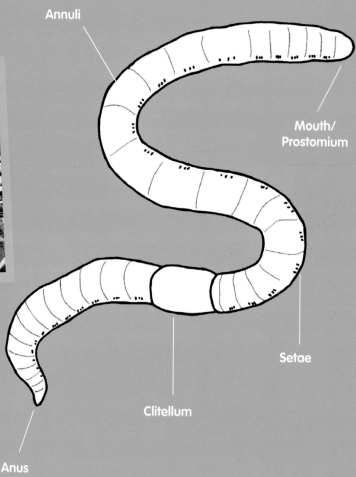

Annuli

Mouth/ Prostomium

Setae

Clitellum

Anus

You wouldn't be alone thinking worms are just slimy bits of fat spaghetti, but they really are amazing incredible creatures.

Earthworms have a flexible skeleton that keeps its shape from the fluid running through the worm's muscles. Their organs fill up with water and push out, creating a turgid structure on the outside of their bodies.

They have a very special skeleton, called a HYDROSTATIC SKELETON.

Ha – a bit like a fire hose.

Earthworms are equipped with tiny bristles on their sides and belly called **chaeta**. Each ringed segment is called an **annulus**. Depending on the species, earthworms can have up to 150 annuli. Each annuli have four pairs of bristles protruding from it, called **setae**.

WOW, did you know that earthworms can have their body severed and then regrow their body parts again? I wish we could do that!

Did you know that an earthworm can consume its body weight in one day?

When earthworm muscles contract and elongate the setae bristles grab the ground like tiny ice picks, which helps them grip especially when it's wet and slimy, so they essentially pull themselves through soil.

Earthworms are regarded as environmental engineers and they do such a fabulous job. Remember every animal has a job to do and earthworms are no exception. Worms eat organic waste, and they poop it out in worm castings, releasing important elements into our soil such as magnesium, calcium, phosphorus and nitrogen. These elements are extremely important for plant health and growth.

Did you know that earthworms don't just have one heart, they have five?

As they burrow through the soil they create wormholes, creating microhabitats for other microorganisms. They need their skin to stay wet and slimy for this exchange of oxygen to be efficient, and for them to remain healthy.

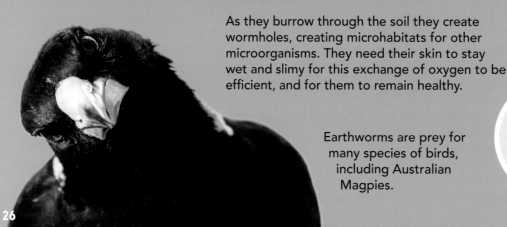

Earthworms are prey for many species of birds, including Australian Magpies.

Did you know that earthworms breathe through their skin? Wow, that's incredible!

The thicker saddle segment is called a **clitellum,** and this is where worms produce their eggs.

Their long tube-like body is the perfect shape for living in and building tunnels. They use the muscles surrounding each annulus to squeeze their body into tight spaces and push themselves into a little gap. Then they use those same muscles to push outwards and make that gap bigger. To ensure the tunnels don't collapse behind them they secrete a slimy mucus (like snot!) from all over their bodies, this slime coats the walls of their tunnels and makes it harden.

Eggs

Cocoon

Life Cycle

Earthworms have mostly simple life cycles, just with one exception. They are **hermaphrodites** – this means that each earthworm has both male and female reproductive organs. When two adult earthworms mate they both lay eggs in a protective cocoon.

Earthworms have both male and female reproductive body parts. However, they still need a partner to mate with in order to trade sperm and produce eggs. Earthworms can produce between three and eighty cocoons every year; each cocoon holds between one and twenty fertilised eggs which take sixty to ninety days to hatch.

Adult earthworms have a clitellum or a saddle, and this is where they produce their egg sac, called a **cocoon**. The cocoon slides off the body of the earthworm and is deposited into the soil.

Young earthworms will then hatch from their eggs and emerge from the cocoon, looking just like the adults but smaller and with less rings or annuli. As the earthworms mature, they'll develop more annuli and eventually their reproductive organs when they reach their adult life stage.

Young

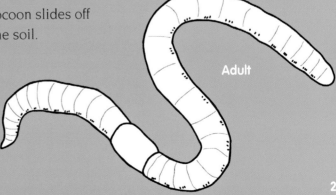

Adult

Predators

Apart from staying underground most earthworms don't have many defences to protect them from predators. Earthworms can be eaten by small mammals, birds, lizards, amphibians and even other invertebrates such as centipedes or spiders.

What can we do to help earthworms?

Earthworms are regarded as an environmental engineer; they do such a fabulous job. Remember every animal has a job to do and earthworms are no exception.

So, kids if you see an earthworm on the footpath, don't squish on it, make sure to put them back into the safety of the garden or they might not survive.

Why not create a worm farm in your home, backyard or even at school? It's heaps of fun and so easy to do. Earthworms are such helpful invertebrates, and will help recycle your household green waste, turning it into super-charged nutrients for your plants and garden.

Guess what? It's free!

Next time you see a worm out and about, please remember that every animal has a job to do and earthworms are no exception. Treat them with respect and help them out. After all they help us out too, and they are such an important part of the food web in so many different ecosystems.

SCAN HERE
to watch a WILD clip

lrjlgs

Garden Slater

Porcellio scaber

'It has a pouch just like a kangaroo!'

This common invertebrate has many confusing and often misleading names. In fact, scientists believe that the Garden Slater has the most regional common names of any living creature. These include wood louse, wood pig, pill bug, roly-poly and butchy boy, to name just a few!

Classification

KINGDOM:	Animalia
PHYLUM:	Arthropoda
CLASS:	Malacostraca
ORDER:	Isopoda
FAMILY:	Porcellionidae
GENUS:	*Porcellio*
SPECIES:	*scaber*

What's in a name?

Who would have thought? Garden Slaters, also known as Common Slaters, are **isopods** originally from aquatic environments which have evolved to live in terrestrial habitats. Isopods have a hard **exoskeleton** and do not have a backbone.

The literal meaning in Greek is *iso* meaning 'equal' and *pod* meaning 'feet', referring to having legs equal in size and position.

Erroneously they are often called 'slater bugs', but they are not insects at all. Having seven pairs of legs, these moisture-loving crustaceans are related to crabs, lobsters and prawns.

Their species name *scaber* means 'rough and scaly'.

Where is it found?

The Garden Slater is a cosmopolitan invertebrate with European ancestry, which has been brought to Australia in the last couple of hundred years. Today it is the most widespread slater species in Australia. Scientists believe there are over 3,500 different species worldwide.

Everyone is familiar with the Garden Slater! This common isopod is a moisture-loving nocturnal species. Because of their permeable exoskeleton, they can lose body water very quickly and dehydrate. The best place to find them is under moist rocks, logs and rotting vegetation.

Slaters are scavengers that feed opportunistically on decaying matter. They fill a fantastic ecological niche as they assist in recycling nutrients and helping to build the soil.

Damp woody places make excellent habitat for slaters.

Don't be scared if Garden Slaters occasionally come into your house. Their elongated flattened bodies help to make them exceptionally skilled at squeezing into tiny places. Never fear, a slater can't bite or sting you – they are totally harmless to people. If you see one, please pick it up gently and place it back outside to continue the great work that they do.

We call them detritivores. Who would have thought that such a small creature has such a BIG job to do?

Amazing adaptations and morphology

These armour-plated crustaceans protect themselves from attack by curling up into a ball just like an armadillo! This makes it much harder to be grabbed by a hungry predator. Curling into a ball also protects the slater from extreme temperatures.

Antennae

Eye

Head

Thorax

Abdomen

Uropod

Did you know that Garden Slaters will feign death, 'playing possum' when threatened or disturbed?

Just like their aquatic ancestors they use gills to breathe, however they will drown if placed in water.

They have eyes on each side of their head. Each eye is comprised of 25 ocelli, which helps them to detect large objects. They have an armour-plated 'tank-like' body divided into seven body segments, seven pairs of jointed limbs and two pairs of antennae.

A slater will shed its skin as it grows larger. However, they don't shed their entire skin in one go, they slough the rear half first and then the front half a couple of days later. During moulting, the slater is highly vulnerable to predators and desiccation, and must find shelter or perish.

Slaters can move surprisingly fast. They are **poikilothermic** and their speed of movement is dependent on their surrounding environmental temperature.

They have two 'tail-like' uropods at the end of their bodies, which help them to find their way about.

That's kind of like a cat's whiskers.

Hey, that's much cheaper than going down to the shops to buy new clothes.

Slaters can excrete ammonia through their exoskeleton to ward off predators.

Ooooooh ,YUK! – eating a slater would be disgusting.

A slater's grey colour helps them to camouflage superbly. A large group of slaters is called a **colony**.

35

...**slaters** have been known to eat their own excrement – yes, poooo!

This behaviour is known as **coprophagia**. They adopt this peculiar behaviour to recycle copper in their diet, as their blood is copper based like marine crustaceans. Copper as a trace element is not always readily available.

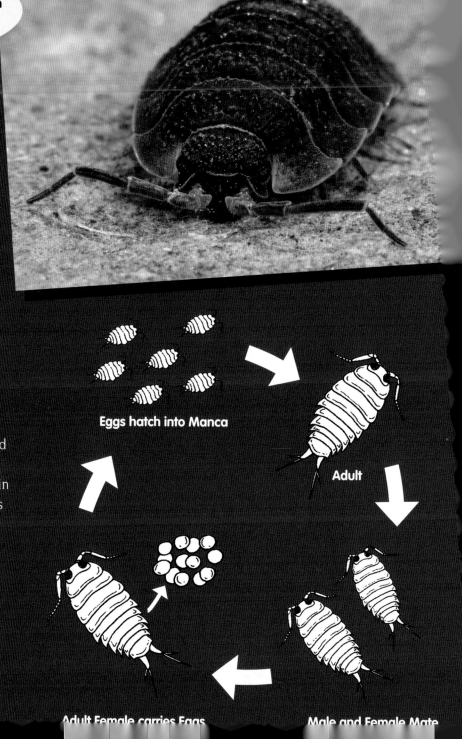

Life cycle

This curious land crustacean can lay up to 90 eggs per brood and can reproduce multiple times in one year. Eggs hatch in the marsupium and the babies remain there for two weeks.

Eggs hatch into Manca

Adult

Adult Female carries Eggs

Male and Female Mate

The Garden Slater carries its eggs in a fluid-filled **marsupium**, a small brood pouch on the underside of its body, and provides developing embryos with water, oxygen and nutrients. When the babies emerge from the pouch they shed their skin twice before growing the seventh pair of limbs.

The young slater is fully grown by three months. They usually live for two years.

Did you know that a baby slater is called a **manca**? Baby slaters look very similar to adults, however they have one less body segment and pair of legs.

Hey WOW, that's just like a marsupial kangaroo!

Predators and threats

Slaters fall easy prey to birds, lizards, spiders, centipedes and even predatory beetles. Try to avoid using insecticides in your garden as this will affect slaters and negatively impact on predators which eat this species.

Small insectivorous birds such as the Superb Fairy-wren like to feast on slaters.

What can we do to help slaters?

- Create habitat for this endearing land crustacean – they favour moist places with rotting vegetation. Why not create a slater hotel?
- In large numbers slaters can be annoying and frustrating as they do eat young and emerging plants. However, learn to live them, as like earthworms they are extremely effective recyclers, breaking down organic waste and returning nutrients back into the soil.

SCAN HERE to watch a WILD clip

mmlbqf

Giant Rainforest Mantid

Hierodula majuscula

'The praying assassin.'

The genus name **Hierodula** is derived from Ancient Greek slaves called the Hierodules – they were dedicated slaves who worshipped God. The species name **majuscula** means 'large' in Latin. In Ancient Greek **mantis** means 'prophet'.

KINGDOM:	Animalia
PHYLUM:	Arthropoda
CLASS:	Insecta
ORDER:	Mantodea
FAMILY:	Mantidae
GENUS:	*Hierodula*
SPECIES:	*majuscula*

What's in a name?

Looking like a character from *Star Wars*, this stealthy carnivorous insect has a voracious appetite and gets the family name **praying mantid** from their front pair of limbs which are shaped like it's in prayer.

Hey, they really do look like they are praying in church!

Where is it found?

The Giant Rainforest Mantid is found in warm tropical northern Queensland. It generally prefers rainforest environments, however it can even be found living in peoples' backyards! A true master of camouflage, this cryptic insect can be found camouflaged in amongst the foliage of trees and shrubs, usually hanging from a branch, always on high alert for smaller invertebrate prey.

These mantids are found in tropical rainforests in north Queensland.

Adult females can grow up to ten centimetres in length, making them one of the largest mantids in the world.

Amazing morphology and adaptations

Giant Rainforest Mantids are extremely powerful and **carnivorous** in nature. They will hunt down insects and other invertebrates for dinner. Incredibly, they have even been recorded to eat small lizards and frogs!

Although harmless to people, Giant Rainforest Mantids can give you quite a painful surprise if picked up roughly, grabbing soft skin in their powerful barbed forelimbs. **OUCH!**

Giant Rainforest Mantids do not have a sting or venom. However, they can still overpower prey much larger than them. For their size they are incredibly powerful – they ambush their prey and simply start eating it.

Mantids are of course insects. They have six legs in three pairs. The front pair of legs are armed with spikes for efficiently grabbing and ensnaring their prey.

These mantids have three distinct body parts: the **head**, **thorax** and **abdomen**. The thorax in this species is purple underneath. A pair of **antennae** protrude from the head. They expertly preen their long antennae, kind of like a cat cleaning its whiskers.

This is one feisty bug that certainly means business.

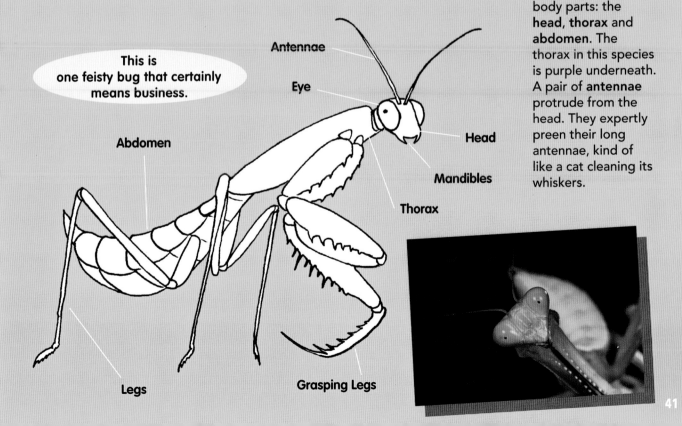

Antennae

Eye

Abdomen

Head

Mandibles

Thorax

Legs

Grasping Legs

WOW... Did you know that mantids have FIVE EYES?

The most obvious are the two large prominent **compound eyes** which detect movement and depth vision, whilst the three smaller **simple eyes** in the middle of the head are used to detect light.

Mantids have the ability to spin their head a full 180 degrees to detect their prey, making them one formidable insect predator.

That is like something out of a creepy horror movie.

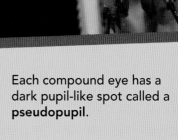

Each compound eye has a dark pupil-like spot called a **pseudopupil.**

That is one cool adaptation – predators are less likely to eat you if they always feel like they are being watched!

A mantid's fat abdomen is filled with energy and fat reserves. This is a great adaptation for when food is scarce, and they can still survive off this fat reserve.

Hey, that's kind of like an in-built bento school lunch box!

Their luminescent lime-green body colour helps them to expertly blend in with their environment.

The female Giant Rainforest Mantid does not fly, possessing vestigial or remnant wings, preferring to climb, whereas the male of this species has larger wings and can fly. This species is gender dimorphic, meaning that there is a noticeable difference in the size and shape of the male and female. The female is much larger, and the male is smaller with noticeably longer wings.

Nymph

Did you know that a baby mantid is called a nymph?

Ootheca

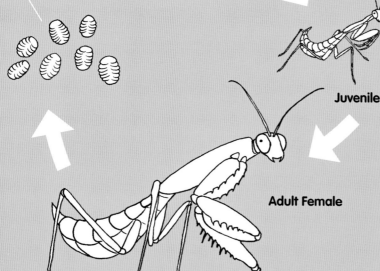

Juvenile

Adult Female

Life Cycle

The Giant Rainforest Mantid is a relatively long-lived insect and can live up to one year. To reproduce the male and female mate, however the larger female mantid is notoriously famous for eating her boyfriend! Scientists believe that they gorge themselves on this tasty opportunity to ensure adequate energy supplies to help produce their eggs. Even if the male is decapitated, mating will still be successful.

Boy oh boy! That is brutal speed dating... yet fascinating.

Approximately twenty to forty days after mating the female produces a foamy mass encapsulating the eggs called an **ootheca**.

It reminds me of hardened fizzy foaming soft drink.

Nymphs freshly hatched from the ootheca.

The ootheca hardens and protects the developing young. The female mantid attaches the ootheca to a branch or bark of a tree.

The developing young can 'overwinter' in torpor in the cooler months, and hatch with the onset of warmer weather, when there is more plentiful food.

The young hatch and emerge after forty to fifty days. Unbelievably up to two hundred babies can hatch from one brood.

Nymphs love to eat fruit flies and other tiny prey. Nature can be brutal, and they are also known to be **cannibalistic** and will eat their siblings.

Hey, I thought that growing up in my family with my siblings was tough!

It's like going up a size in a pair of jeans.

As the young nymph develops and grows, it sheds its skin. This is called **ecdysis**. Each growth stage is called an **instar**.

Threats and Predators

Loss of suitable habitat and the use of chemicals and pesticides have all negatively impacted on the Giant Rainforest Mantid.

Many Australian animal species, such as kookaburras, butcherbirds and frilled lizards, would relish a snack in the form of a juicy mantid. Domestic dogs and cats will also easily consume these beautiful insects.

Nocturnal birds such as the Tawny Frogmouth will feed on mantids.

What can we do to help mantids?

- Every animal has a job to do and an important ecological niche. Mantids are no exception – they eat up all the bugs and maintain balance in our ecosystems. So why not create some habitat and plant a few native shrubs in your backyard or school yard, welcoming mantids into your life?
- Lastly, be responsible pet owners, and keep your pet enclosed so it doesn't gobble up native wildlife.

They really are one super cool insect.

SCAN HERE
to watch a WILD clip

tekjyw

Millipede

Order Spirobolida

'The leggiest of all invertebrates.'

What's in a name?

The word millipede is derived from the Latin *milli*, meaning 'thousand', and *pede*, meaning 'feet'.

Did you know that the first 'true-to-its-name' millipede was only just recently discovered here in Australia? The female *Eumillipes persephone* has 1,306 legs.

Some people think that millipedes actually have a million legs – that's simply not true.

Eumillipes now has the title of being the world's leggiest creature.

Classification

KINGDOM:	Animalia
PHYLUM:	Arthropoda
SUBPHYLUM:	Myriapoda
CLASS:	Diplopoda
ORDER:	Spirobolida

Millipedes live in a wide range of very different habitats, including rainforests.

Where are they found?

Many different millipede species can be found in moist forests and woodlands throughout Australia. They are generally nocturnal, hiding beneath soil, leaf litter and rotting vegetation in the daytime. Australia is home to more than two thousand different species, for example the Giant Scrub Millipede which prefers warm and humid environments in tropical Queensland. You are most probably familiar with the small, black, shiny and abundant Spanish Millipede. It was introduced to the southern states of Australia and now in ubiquitous feral fashion has become an agricultural pest.

And boy oh boy, they sure can stink!

With very few predators the Spanish Millipede can rapidly build up in numbers. So much so that in April 2002 this mini arthropod actually stopped the train service from Melbourne to Ballarat.

A plague of millipedes, and their sheer numbers squashed on the track, left train wheels unable to gain traction in their oily squishy stinky goo.

Millipedes are of course arthropods with many, many, many, many legs.

They remind me of council street-cleaning machines.

Some species of millipedes curl up into a ball to protect themselves from changes in environmental conditions or as a defence against predators, protecting their soft vulnerable underside.

Interestingly, millipedes breathe through their sides. Air passes through trachea near their legs and on to the tracheal system.

Amazing morphology and adaptations

Millipedes have a highly segmented body with two pairs of jointed legs on each body segment. The number of legs varies between the many different species found.

The legs of a millipede are divided into seven joints. Males have longer legs than females.

The **Giant Scrub Millipede** has a rounded body with a hard exoskeleton. Millipede exoskeletons have a waxy coating (**cuticle**), which enables them to reduce the amount of water they lose to the external environment. Each of their body segments is called a **tergite**. As these amazing creatures walk, each pair of legs is lifted at the same time, transporting them along like a 'Mexican wave'.

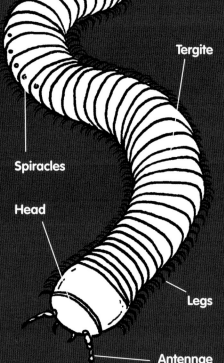

Tergite

Spiracles

Head

Legs

Antennae

Pooooo-weeee, it smells like iodine to me. That's disgusting. Urgggh!

A millipede's heart is as long as its body... Whoooah, that's HUGE.

If threatened millipedes can exude a noxious-smelling fluid from their sides. This foul secretion is composed of organic chemicals called **quinones** and exuded through **ozopores** in the skin. This defence strategy would make them distasteful for any would-be predator.

Millipedes have extremely poor eyesight; some scientists believe that they can't see at all. They use their short antennae to feel their way about, continually tapping the ground...

A bit like a sight-impaired person with a cane.

They are extremely clean creatures; they spend hour upon hour cleaning and polishing their bodies. Millipedes have specially adapted cleaning legs on their second or third body segment which help them to clean their antennae.

When they crawl and burrow they eat their way through the decaying vegetation and fungi. Millipedes are extremely effective **detritivores**, recycling and unlocking nutrients back into the soil.

Did you know that certain species of primates have learnt to squish up millipedes and rub the juices all over their fur... the smell acts as an excellent insect repellent. Who needs Aerogard? – LOL!

Life Cycle

Millipedes are **hemimetabolous**. This means that they don't have a pupa life stage. Instead, they only have three life stages: egg, nymph and adult.

Millipedes begin life as an egg, hidden in the moist leaf litter or soil. The eggs hatch and a tiny millipede nymph will emerge.

The nymph is only born with three pairs of legs. As they grow they shed their exoskeleton. Each time they slough their outer skin more body segments and legs are formed.

Millipedes continually grow and shed their skin until they have reached maturity and adult body size.

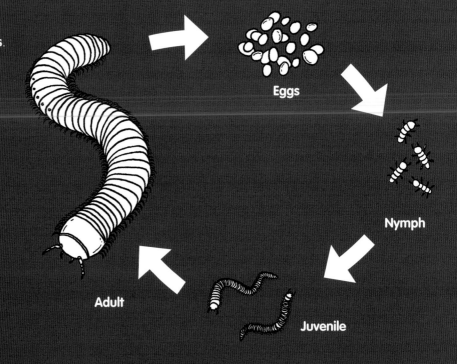

Eggs

Nymph

Adult

Juvenile

How can we help millipedes?

They are fantastic for our environment, breaking down organic waste and recycling nutrients back into the soil. That's great for our natural world and great for us.

Why not do some mulching this weekend and create a perfect environment for

Threats and predators

In Australia, millipedes are abund[...] making them potentially easy prey for predators. However, the toxins they secrete through their skin offe[...] exceptional protection from attack[...] most animals prefer to avoid them.

Mammals such as bandicoot[s] include millipedes in their diets.

It makes sense doesn't it? Next time you see a millipede, don't whack it or squish it. Leave it alone and let it do its job.

They can't harm us; they do a great job... and they are fascinating to watch.

SCAN HERE
to watch a WILD clip

wqhqfk

Centipede

'A nimble ballerina with fangs!'

Family Scolopendridae

This prehistoric-looking 'creepy crawly' has been around for 430 million years. They can be found almost everywhere on the planet and they are well known for being voracious venomous predators! The largest centipede in Australia is the Giant Centipede, which can reach sixteen centimetres long – that's over half a ruler length.

What's in a name?

Centipedes belong to the Arthropod class of animals Chilopoda. The Latin translation refers to the Greek word **kheilos**, meaning 'lip', and **pous** or **pod**, meaning 'foot'. The class name refers to the menacing claws on their first pair of legs. These grabbing claws are formidable weapons and enable them to inject venom into their prey. The word centipede refers to having one hundred legs, however this is incorrect, the number of legs varies between the many different species.

Where are they found?

Giant centipedes can be found all over Australia. They are more numerous in the tropical and subtropical forests of northern Australia, and can often be found in suburban gardens when logs, rocks and vegetation are disturbed. Situations such as this are where most centipede bites occur.

Almost any habitat can be home to giant centipedes, but they do have a few places they prefer to live. They can be found in forests, leaf litter, rocky areas, sand and even in cliffs! Although an encounter with a giant centipede can be terrifying for many people, these arthropods will always try to escape rather than fight.

Many habitats in Australia hold giant centipedes, from rainforest to dry open woodland.

I have actually been bitten by a large centipede, and YIKES I felt thumping excruciating pain... it was like my hand was being hit by a hammer and felt like it was on fire.

The last pair of legs are longer, thicker and point backwards.

The first pair of legs are equipped with venomous claws. They are called the **forcipules**.

Hey, they are a runner not a fighter. LOL!

Amazing morphology and adaptations

Giant centipedes have some special adaptations to help them to survive, including **nocturnal behaviour** to avoid the hot desiccating sun during the day.

Centipedes have flattened bodies with one pair of legs per body segment.

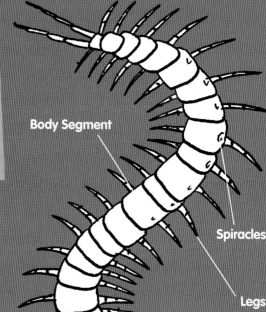

Body Segment

Spiracles

Legs

Head

Forcipule/Venom Claw

Ocelli/Eyes

Antennae

When threatened or attacked, centipedes often wiggle wildly and wave their back legs upwards, pretending they have two heads.

What a clever adaptation. A predator would be less likely to eat a centipede with two heads – that would be double trouble!

The venom is used to subdue prey and assist with digestion. They have two simple eyes called **ocelli** – they can detect light and dark with these eyes.

They are equipped with long flat bodies which enable them to easily squeeze into tight cracks to catch their prey, or retreat from the sun.

Unlike you and I, breathing through our nostrils and mouth, centipedes breathe through small holes along the sides of their body call **spiracles**.

Centipede bodies are incredibly strong, and flexible! Like a 'ballerina assassin', they can move quickly, twisting and turning to capture their prey!

A centipede has a head with a pair of sensory antennae, and three pairs of jaws. Inside the mouth is a pair of salivary glands which they use to secrete a fluid to groom their legs and antennae.

WOW, that beats buying expensive body wash and shampoo… just spit on yourself why don't you!

The centipede has relatively poor vision. In its dark subterranean world it relies on touch – sensory feet and hairs attached to nerve fibres enable them to feel their way about their environment.

A centipede's last pair of legs might look a bit strange pointing backwards, but they use them to grab and hold onto their prey. They also point them up into the air to scare away predators, that's called a **bluff** mechanism!

The centipede's back is covered in body armour.

Centipedes have one pair of legs on each armoured body segment. These legs stick out from their sides, unlike their millipede cousins whose legs are protected underneath the body.

The segmented legs are equipped with 'icepick'-like claws for masterfully gripping and climbing efficiently across their terrestrial world.

That's because they grow special plates along their back to protect them, called **TERGITES**.

Centipedes are incredibly nimble and dextrous. Having so many legs enables them to vary footholds and traverse the ground surprisingly quickly. Only one out of eight of the centipede's legs touch the ground at any one time.

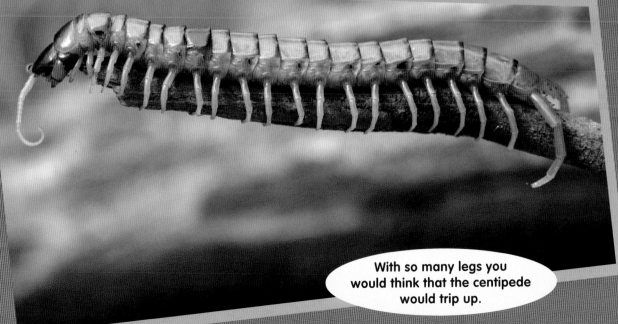

With so many legs you would think that the centipede would trip up.

Life Cycle

Giant centipedes are **oviparous**, which means that they reproduce by laying eggs.

Centipedes reproduce without touch. Female centipedes emit pheromones to advertise their willingness to breed. A male suitor produces a spermatophore and places it for the female to insert into her reproductive region, to fertilise her eggs.

The mother centipede will lay up to thirty eggs at once! The protective female will also curl around her eggs to protect them.

When the young centipedes hatch, they already have all their legs and body segments. They look just like tiny adult centipedes. This is known as **epimorphic development.**

The young centipedes will stay with their mother until they have shed their exoskeleton twice. After that they are big enough to protect themselves. They must shed their exoskeleton around ten times before they are fully grown.

Eggs

Juveniles

Adult

Predators and Threats

Centipedes are of course predators themselves, however they can still be predated upon by other animals. A centipede would be no match for a hungry sand monitor lizard, bearded dragon, or even a kookaburra. Cleverly, if they lose any legs they can regrow them next time they shed their exoskeleton.

What can we do to help centipedes?

- Remember, next time you see a centipede don't 'squish' it – leave it alone and it will leave you alone.
- Centipedes are such important insect predators; they help to keep the balance in our natural world.
- Perhaps you could create some habitat for a centipede in your backyard or school playground.

Reptiles such as bearded dragons will feed on centipedes.

Imagine if we didn't have centipedes – there would be insects everywhere.

Why not place down some logs, rocks and natural vegetation, and create a home for our 'leggy friend'. Remember, they were here first, and they deserve our respect.

SCAN HERE
to watch a WILD clip

tumasg

61

Australian Tarantula

Family Theraphosidae

'The stuff of nightmares for some.'

What's in a name?

Funnily enough, the word tarantula is derived from a seaport town of Taranto in southern Italy. The name was originally given to a species of wolf spider, Lycosa tarantula. One bite from this feared arachnid apparently caused crazed symptoms of weeping and wild jerky movements. The Tarantella dance was born in Italian folk dancing – it is also called 'the dance of the spider'.

The quick and often jerky movement of the tarantula is enough to make anyone jump.

Australian tarantulas are considered primitive spiders and belong to an infraorder of spiders known as **mygalomorphs**. They prefer to live in a burrow beneath the ground.

Unlike Charlotte, in *Charlotte's Web*, who likes to spin a web and trap her food.

Australian tarantulas have a variety of common names, in particular the name **bird-eating spider** is highly over-exaggerated.

HA! Anyhow, they should be called a bird-drinking spider as they don't eat their food like you and I do – essentially they suck the juices out of their food.

They are often referred to as **whistling** or **barking spiders**, as some specimens can make a raspy whistling sound by rubbing their mouthparts together when threatened. This behaviour is called **stridulating**.

Classification

KINGDOM:	Animalia
PHYLUM:	Arthropoda
CLASS:	Arachnida
ORDER:	Araneae
INFRAORDER:	Mygalomorphae
FAMILY:	Theraphosidae

Where is it found?

Tarantulas are **burrowing** animals, which means they like to dig tunnels underground. This means they are **subterranean.** They use leaf litter, soil and tree bark to disguise the entrances to their burrows.

Adult females may dig a burrow up to two metres deep, but young spiders may choose to live anywhere, such as under rocks or tree roots, until they are bigger.

Tarantulas are widespread and live in warmer parts of Australia. They can be found in rainforests, deserts and savannah grasslands. Often they can be seen after heavy downpours and flooding, when their subterranean lair has been inundated with water.

Tarantulas are usually **nocturnal,** which means they come out at night to hunt. They have been known to eat a variety of insects, lizards and even frogs.

Savannah grasslands of outback Australia are home to these spiders.

Hey, that's like a spider disco dance!

Life Cycle

Tarantulas are **oviparous,** which means that they reproduce by laying eggs. The mother spins a little sac out of silk from her **spinnerets**. This is where she keeps her eggs safe in her burrow.

During the warmer months of the year the male will approach the female's burrow to entice her out to breed. The smaller male must show his willingness to mate, instead of being potential prey for the female, by patting his palps, which are his reproductive organs, on the ground and then on the female's body.

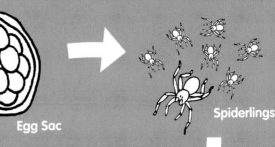

Egg Sac

Spiderlings

Adult

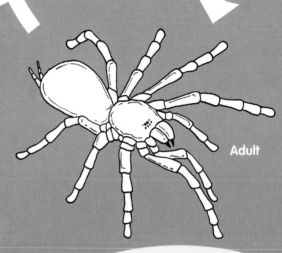

The female will rear up and the male will place his palps into her reproductive opening before making a hasty escape! If a successful mating occurs the female will lay an egg sac and carefully cover it with spider silk. There could be up to 100 eggs deposited inside. The female will carefully safeguard and care for the eggs until they hatch.

Mum tarantulas have been known to help their brood of babies find food, by placing dead insects next to them.

Wow, that really is motherly love.

Hey, do you want to hear a gory fact? There is a species of tarantula in South Africa that allows its offspring to eat it alive. That's called matriphagy. What a sacrifice!

The eggs hatch after about 38 days into babies called spiderlings. These are very small babies so they have a lot of growing to do.

When they start to grow, they must shed their old **exoskeletons**. Just like when you get rid of your old clothes when you grow bigger!

The spiderlings grow very quickly and only spend a couple of days with their mother.

Females can live for up to twelve years. Males usually die within twelve months after mating.

Amazing morphology and adaptations

Australian tarantulas are animals which belong to the class Arachnida.

Unlike insects, which have three body parts, arachnids have only two. The head and thorax are fused together into a **cephalothorax** and the large 'lunch box' behind is called the **abdomen**. You can clearly see their spinnerets, which they use to create silk to make a web.

Let's break down the classification of a spider, shall we? Can you see its two body parts?

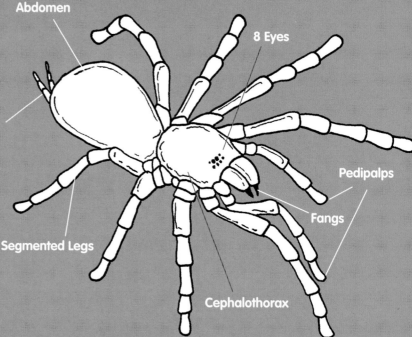

Abdomen

8 Eyes

Spinnerets

Pedipalps

Fangs

Segmented Legs

Cephalothorax

The eight segmented legs of the tarantula have **retractable claws** that assist it with climbing and adhering to surfaces.

Hey, they have something in common with a household cat.

In addition to their eight legs, they have what appears to be a pair of shorter legs called the **pedipalps**. In between the pedipalps are the **chelicerae** which have fangs at the end.

WARNING: tarantulas are venomous and should not be handled. Although there are no records of deaths from a tarantula bite in Australia, bites are extremely painful and can cause extreme swelling, necrosis and vomiting.

Tarantulas communicate with each other by **stridulating** – rubbing their stiff body parts against another surface to make a noise to attract a mate or to ward off a potential threat.

That's like a 'spidery' way to snapchat or text.

Many tarantula bodies and appendages are covered in fine sensory hairs, to help them sense their environment, to aid movement, and to detect prey.

Australian tarantulas have **eight eyes** grouped together in pairs. Usually there are two larger eyes in the middle of their head, and these are surrounded by three eyes on either side.

That's FOUR pairs of sunglasses you'd have to wear to the beach!

There's no need to shave your legs when you are a spider – hairy legs come in handy.

Predators and Threats

Believe it or not Australian tarantulas are highly sought-after captives in the pet industry, often commanding very high prices to purchase. The high demand has caused some unscrupulous collectors to decimate many tarantula populations. Wild tarantulas are now protected by law in many states and collection is only allowed under a regulated permit system. Pet tarantulas should be sourced from captive-bred livestock.

Sand Goannas are predators of tarantulas.

What can we do to help tarantulas?

Remember, next time you see a spider don't 'squish' it – leave it alone and it will leave you alone.

Spiders of all species are such important insect predators. They help to keep the balance in our natural world.

Perhaps you could create some habitat for spiders in your backyard?

Next time an eight-legged friend wanders into your home, don't squish it, gently capture it or shoo it outside. Remember, they were here first, they eat up all of the bugs and deserve our respect.

Imagine if we didn't have spiders – there would be insects everywhere.

SCAN HERE to watch a WILD clip

nfucfn

69

Flinders Ranges Scorpion

Urodacus elongatus

'One of Australia's largest scorpion species!'

Classification

KINGDOM:	Animalia
PHYLUM:	Arthropoda
CLASS:	Chelicerata
ORDER:	Scorpiones
FAMILY:	Scorpionidae
GENUS:	Urodacus
SPECIES:	*elongatus*

What's in a name?

The species name *elongatus* refers to this species' noticeably long tail. **Scorpiones** is derived from the Greek word **scorpios**, meaning 'to cut', referring to this animal's pincer-like chelicerae (mouth parts).

Australia is home to over one hundred species of scorpion and the Flinders Ranges Scorpion is one of the largest. Although Australian scorpions can be venomous, no species is considered life threatening to humans, however some scorpions in other countries can kill!

If you do get bitten by a scorpion, always seek immediate medical attention.

Where is it found?

As the name suggests, this large ground-dwelling terrestrial arachnid lives in the sandy foothills, dry riverbeds and rocky outcrops of South Australia's Flinders Ranges. It needs a moist microhabitat, preferring a scrape underneath a rock to shelter in during the heat of the day.

The Flinders Ranges in South Australia.

Amazing morphology and adaptations

Solely a carnivore, this voracious predator is a nocturnal hunter of a wide range of arthropods, eating cockroaches, slaters, spiders, insects, centipedes and millipedes. Scorpions have an extraordinarily low metabolism and can survive on as little as **one meal a month**.

> Woah, I think I would have a very grumbly tummy.

Of course, scorpions are **arthropods**, which means that they have an **exoskeleton**, a segmented body and paired jointed appendages. Arachnids have two body parts, called the cephalothorax and the abdomen, and eight jointed legs! The cephalothorax contains the mouth parts, eyes, pedipalps and legs.

This arachnid ambush predator has some amazing features.

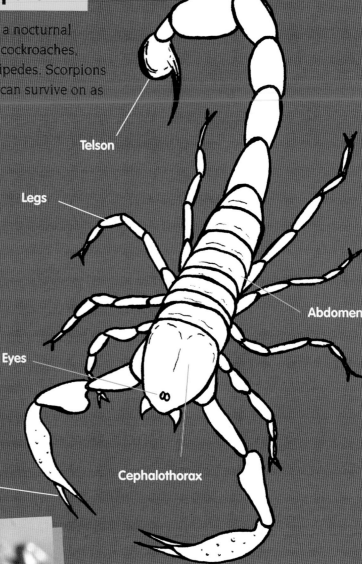

Telson

Legs

Abdomen

Eyes

Cephalothorax

Pincers

> It's like an army tank with all of the weaponry. It would be the stuff of nightmares for a poor unsuspecting bug.

Did you know that scorpions are related to spiders, mites and ticks?

WOW, I love learning new scientific words.

They have a long tail, which is also called a metasoma. At the end of the tail is a venomous barbed stinger called the telson.

They have long arms called pedipalps, equipped with 'crab-like' pincers for grabbing.

Flinders Ranges Scorpions are an excellent ambush predator, patiently waiting at the entrance of their lair for an unsuspecting victim to stroll past. The scorpion then grabs the prey with its claws and envenomates it.

A ruthless predator of the invertebrate world... yikes, what a way to go!

Incredibly, Flinders Ranges Scorpions fluoresce in ultraviolet light. Scientists believe that this fluorescence acts as a UV-sensitive adaptation, to help the scorpion avoid damaging light levels and desiccation.

Uniquely, scorpions are equipped with a pair of sensory organs on their underside called **pectines**, which help them to pick up and analyse ground texture and scents.

That is so cool – they glow in the dark like Kryptonite!

Amazing – they're like the bloodhound of the invertebrate world.

Life Cycle

Scorpions are unusual amongst invertebrates as they are **ovoviviparous**, which means that the eggs develop and hatch internally and the mother gives birth to live young.

This species of scorpion is gender dimorphic, meaning that there is a noticeable size difference between the male and female. Adult males can reach a whopping twelve centimetres in length, whereas the female, although more 'thick-set', grows to a length of ten centimetres.

The mating ritual of the Flinders Ranges Scorpion is truly monumentally epic! The male and female find each other by scent, vibration and touch.

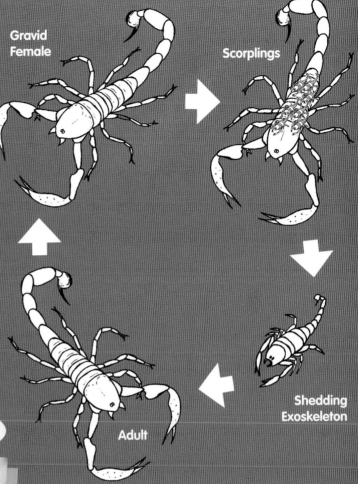

Gravid Female

Scorplings

Shedding Exoskeleton

Adult

The male has a longer tail and there is a very good reason for this. It's due to their amazing courtship and reproduction.

Like out of a scene from a *Transformers* movie, the male and female hold each other at 'arms-length', the male just out of reach of the female's sting.

The longer tail of the male enables him to sting the female to subdue her enough to sneakily deposit his reproductive package (spermatophore) onto the ground beneath the wrestling duo.

This is when the fun begins – they do a scorpion 'waltz' where the package is inserted into the female's reproductive pore. How romantic!

After eighteen months the mother gives birth to babies called **scorplings**. She can have up to fifty babies. The vulnerable youngsters are then 'piggy-backed' around on their mother's back.

Hey, that's like a scorpion creche... what a loving mum!

Flinders Ranges Scorpions are relatively slow at growing, and it will take up to five years before they reach maturity. Some individuals have been recorded to live for a quarter of a century.

Small native mammals such as the Yellow-footed Antechinus will prey on scorpions.

Threat and Predators

Because this species has a restricted range it faces very real threats from tourism. The Flinders Ranges is a popular holiday location for campers. Camping, firewood collecting, habitat loss and foot traffic could directly negatively impact on this amazing species in the future.

The Flinders Ranges Scorpion is also commonly sold in pet shops and online as an alternative pet for creepy-crawly enthusiasts. Illegal collection of this charismatic and 'plucky' invertebrate from the wild could negatively impact this species.

Although venomous, Flinders Ranges Scorpions do have predators. Brown Falcons, Sand Goannas and antechinuses, just to name a few, would all pursue a juicy scorpion for a meal.

What can we do to help scorpions?

Don't harm scorpions. Protect their habitat. Remember, if you leave them alone, they will leave you alone too. Wear sturdy shoes and gloves when working outdoors. Respect scorpions – they have been around for 420 million years!

That's way longer than the dinosaurs. I think that they are incredible survivors – let's look after them together.

SCAN HERE
to watch a WILD clip

zpcuns

Bull Ant

Myrmecia species

'Wingless wasps with a sting that packs a punch!'

These insects are highly aggressive and unpredictable. Also known as 'bulldog ants', bull ants protect themselves with some of the most **toxic venom** in the insect world. Many people are allergic to its bite, which can cause life-threatening anaphylactic shock. At the very least, expect excruciating pain that builds to a deep, throbbing ache. A bite from a bull ant is memorable to say the least, and the pain can last for many days.

A large bull ant can have six times more venom than a honeybee.

What's in a name?

It has always puzzled me how this ant got its name. Maybe it's because they have a fearsome reputation for being aggressive, bold and attacking. That could apply to a bull or a bulldog!

Once bitten, this ferocious ant species is unlikely to let go, hanging on violently with its powerful mandibles. Many members of this genus characteristically jump up and bound about. This is one insect which you don't want to mess with.

Does it bark, or perhaps it's friendly and likes a pat?

The genus name **Myrmecia** refers to the dome-shaped nest of this ant, and it looks like the shape of a certain type of viral wart! Members of the *Myrmecia* genus are one of the most primitive group of ants on Earth. Scientists believe bull ants to be less evolved and sophisticated than other ants as they don't create scent trails or travel in ant lines. The bull ant population in a colony or nest is usually much smaller than that of other species, usually numbering around a hundred individuals, occasionally up to a thousand, whereas other ant species can have millions.

Bull ants have certainly been around for more than 50 million years, and it is quite likely that they bit and stung dinosaurs.

Did you know that bull ants are actually a group of wingless wasps that have adopted to a crawling lifestyle instead?

Classification

KINGDOM:	Animalia
PHYLUM:	Arthropoda
CLASS:	Insecta
ORDER:	Hymenoptera
FAMILY:	Formicidae
GENUS:	*Myrmecia*

Amazing morphology and adaptations

Growing up to four centimetres in length, bull ants are the heavyweights of the Australian ants.

Equipped with long powerful mandibles, these ants are formidable predators. Contrary to popular belief there is no venom in the powerful, sharp, pinching bite.

Bull ants are of course insects with three distinct body parts: the head, thorax and abdomen. The abdomen is where they keep their venomous sting – they use their powerful pinching mandibles to grab their unsuspecting victim, and then curl their abdomen to sting, sometimes multiple times!

The pain from the sting of a bull ant is so intense it rates a 3 out of 4 on the Schmidt sting pain index.

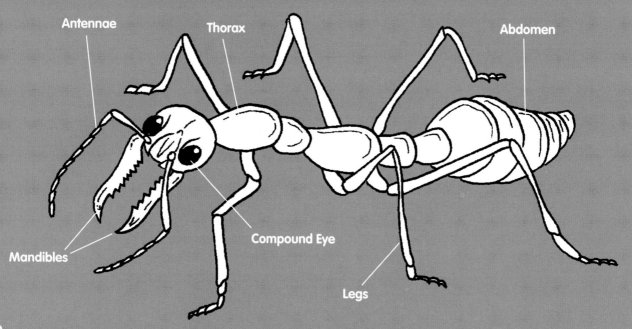

Antennae · Thorax · Abdomen · Mandibles · Compound Eye · Legs

Where are they found?

Bull ants in Australia occur in many varied habitats and environments widespread across the continent. They can be found in urban parklands, coastal areas, forests, woodlands and even deserts. For nesting they favour well-drained open areas. The nest is usually underground, extending over two metres in a subterranean cavern, or in a rotting tree stump, sand, soil or under rocks. Usually seen in the daytime, most bull ant species are diurnal.

Jeepers, you would hate to be Justin Schmidt, the scientist who had to be stung by all of those insects. OUCH!

Bull ants have incredible eyesight and are able to observe and follow movement up to a metre away, enabling them to chase down prey or an intruder from a distance.

WOW, queen ants of some species can live for up to thirty-eight years.

Unlike most other ants, members of this incredible genus use touch and smell to communicate with each other.

Bull ants, like all insects, are **poikilothermic**. The body temperature of an ant is dependent on its external environment. Often when the weather is cooler, bull ants cease activity and shelter in their nest. Cleverly, bull ants are known to adorn the entrance of their nest with heat-absorbing material such as wood and stones, to help increase the ambient temperature around the surrounding area and nest chamber.

What a clever adaptation – it's like solar panels on the roof of your house.

Life Cycle

A colony of bull ants consists of different castes of ants with differing jobs. The varying roles include: the sterile female workers, which forage for food on the ground; fertile females, which can briefly fly and possibly become queens; and the short-lived winged fertile males, which fly in search of a queen to mate with, and then die. Finally, there are the soldiers – their job is to protect the colony.

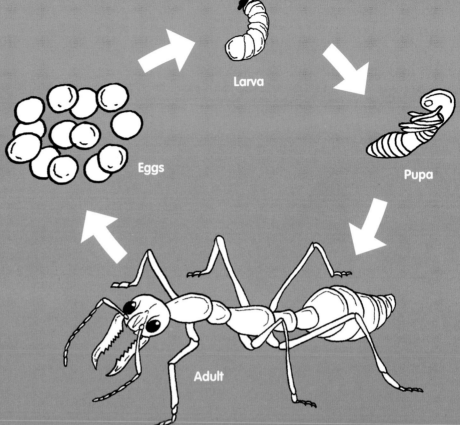

Eggs

Larva

Pupa

Adult

I love this ant – it certainly has a lot of courage and pluck.

She definitely deserves the Mother of the Year Award.

The bull ant's life cycle is in four stages – an egg is laid, a larva hatches, it pupates and the adult emerges. It can take three or four months for an egg to hatch and develop into an adult.

A vast majority of all eggs laid will hatch female. The ants will grow into a particular role – a worker, a soldier or a queen.

Worker bull ants will lay eggs; however, larvae will not develop and hatch. In fact, the infertile eggs are carried off and fed to the developing larvae as a useful form of nutrients.

Bull ant workers can live up three months, but the queen will live much longer. Did you know that the queen bull ant will leave the security of her nest to actively hunt for food for her developing larvae?

Predators and threats

Very few animals are foolhardy enough to consume bull ants with their formidable stings and powerful mandibles. However, the larvae of the developing bull ants are readily consumed by Short-beaked Echidna and small species of burrowing snakes called blind snakes.

Echidnas specialise in feeding on ants.

How can we help bull ants?

Bull ants fill a vital ecological niche and they do a great job. They are important pollinators of many plant species, and their scavenging feeding habits help clean up waste and dead animals.

They really are nature's garbage collectors.

SCAN HERE
to watch a WILD clip

txzyfq

Freshwater Yabby

Cherax destructor

'A survival specialist, enduring years without food or water buried beneath the mud.'

What's in a name?

The Freshwater Yabby's species name **destructor** was derived from its damaging behaviour, by burrowing deep into farmer's dams and levy banks, often causing breaches and sometimes even collapse.

The genus name **Cherax** is thought to be a misspelling of the Ancient Greek word **Charax**, meaning 'pointed stake', which possibly describes the pointed head of this genus.

The common name of the yabby is derived from indigenous people of inland Australia who called it **Yabij.** It was a very important food source for First Nations people.

Who would have thought that a small crustacean could be so destructive?

Where is it found?

Yabbies inhabit freshwater aquatic environments and are Australia's most widespread crayfish. Found in swamps, rivers, streams and dams, they are predominantly nocturnal and feed at night. They are opportunistic scavengers, eating both vegetation and meat. They can even become cannibalistic when conditions are overcrowded.

They are native to the eastern parts of Australia, west of the Great Dividing Range. This yabby has been introduced to many other parts of Australia, and has become an invasive species in Western Australia, outcompeting and negatively impacting on local native freshwater crayfish species.

Yabbies can be found in outback rivers.

Amazing adaptations and morphology

The yabby is equipped with an arsenal of cool adaptations which help it to survive.

Their **exoskeleton** makes them like an armoured vehicle or tank, capable of withstanding attack from a hungry predator.

Amazingly, yabbies have the ability to **regenerate their limbs** when lost. They do this the next time they moult or shed their exoskeleton.

They have two pairs of sensory antennae, allowing them to be acutely aware of changes in their immediate environment.

Equipped with ten main appendages, this freshwater crayfish is no 'push-over'. The yabby is armed with two large and muscular **chelipeds** or 'pincers'. These formidable limbs are used for cutting food, capturing prey and fighting and wrestling other yabbies.

Their large powerful modified legs also assist in deterring rogue male suitors wandering into their territory, who might be trying to steal potential girlfriends. They are excellent weaponry against potential predators.

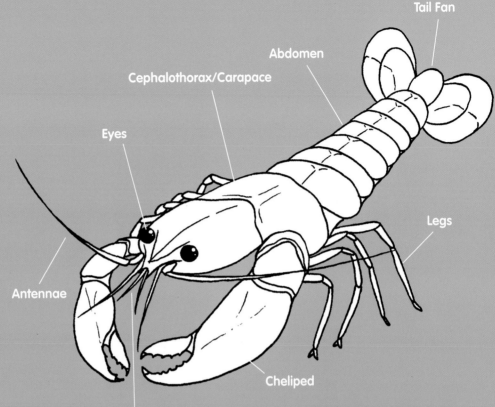

Tail Fan

Abdomen

Cephalothorax/Carapace

Eyes

Legs

Antennae

Cheliped

Antennules

The yabby is highly adaptive to changes in water temperature, being able to tolerate extremes from near freezing to 35 degrees Celsius!

A yabby is a **camouflage** expert, and its colour can be determined partially by the environment in which it lives. They come in many different colours, from greens, to vibrant cobalt blue, to muddy dark brown.

The smaller legs of a yabby have grabbing claws.

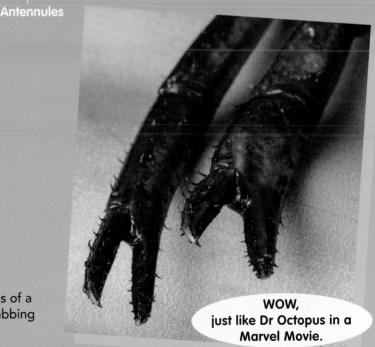

WOW, just like Dr Octopus in a Marvel Movie.

Yabbies are opportunistic **omnivores**, eating both meat and plant matter. They are important **detritivores**, breaking down and consuming waste in freshwater ecosystems.

They are survival experts and are incredibly adaptive, surviving extensive periods of drought by burrowing into the mud and surviving for up to **seven years**! Yabbies crawl into a small moist chamber often metres beneath the ground, practically ceasing normal body functions such as respiration, pulse and digestion, and go into a state of **suspended animation**. This behavioural adaptation is called **aestivation**. Following the onset of rain and preferable wetter conditions, yabbies will travel vast distances in search of a new aquatic home.

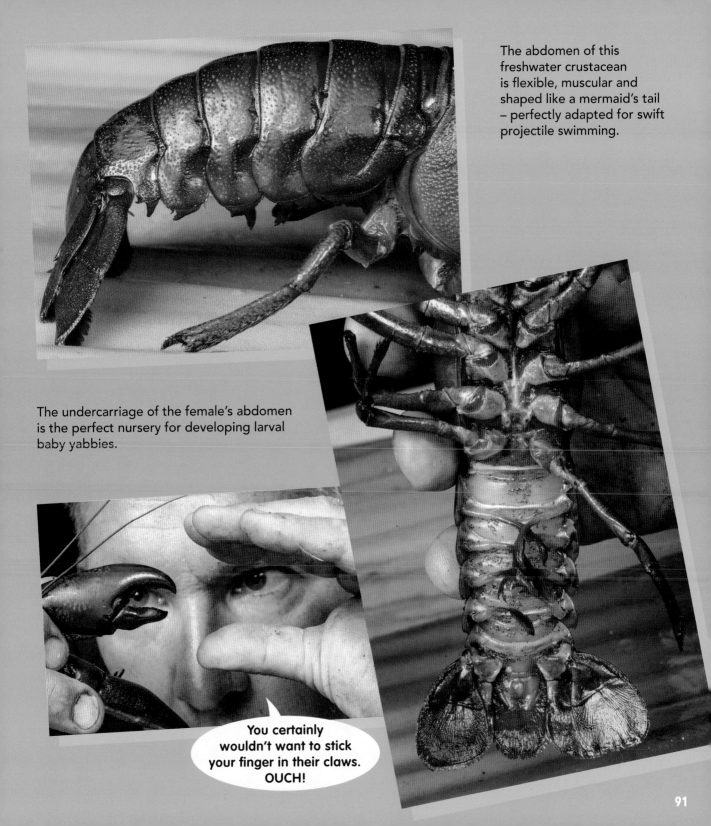

The abdomen of this freshwater crustacean is flexible, muscular and shaped like a mermaid's tail – perfectly adapted for swift projectile swimming.

The undercarriage of the female's abdomen is the perfect nursery for developing larval baby yabbies.

You certainly wouldn't want to stick your finger in their claws. OUCH!

Life Cycle

Yabbies are oviparous and hatch from eggs.

The yabby reproduces in a most peculiar way. A ready-to-breed male yabby presents the female with a reproductive package of sperm gel called a **spermatophore**. He attaches it to the fourth and fifth pair of her legs called **pereopods**. Soon after, the female releases her eggs over the spermatophore, fertilising the eggs. The larval baby yabbies have small hooks on their legs which they attach to the feathery swimmerets or pleopods underneath the female's abdomen.

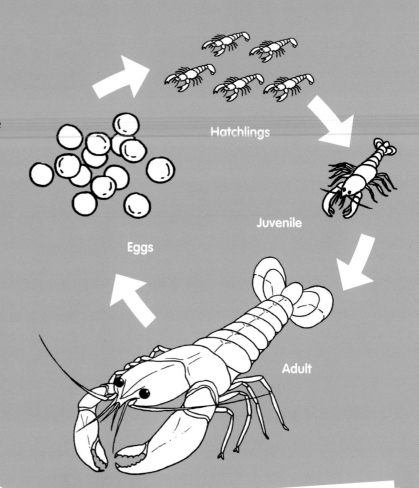

Hatchlings

Juvenile

Eggs

Adult

The number of baby yabbies produced depends on the actual size of the mum. Some larger females can produce up to one thousand young at once! In favourable conditions, baby yabbies moult their skin every couple of days.

Hey, it's like a baby yabby day-care centre!

Predators and threats

Yabbies are an important part of many freshwater ecosystems. Many animals such as platypus, birds, lizards and even White-tailed Water Rats eat them with gusto. People also relish them as food.

The biggest threats to the Freshwater Yabby are extended drought periods associated with climate change, pollution, litter and waste. In particular petrochemicals washing into storm water, rivers and streams negatively impact on the future survival of the yabby. The International Union for Conservation of Nature (IUCN) lists the yabby as vulnerable.

Mammalian predators such as Platypus feed on yabbies.

Next time you go fishing for yabbies, please don't take them all, and throw back the females with eggs.

How can we help yabbies?

Yabbies are highly susceptible to pollution created by humankind.

Make sure that you strive to use environmentally friendly detergents and cleaning products. Be mindful of what you wash down the sink.

Most importantly, please pick up your dog's poo. Next time it rains, pet waste washes into our drains, storm water and waterways, polluting the yabbies' home with harmful nitrogen and phosphorus.

Yabbies help to break down vegetation and rotting waste in our waterways, stopping our wetlands and river systems from becoming polluted and deoxygenated.

SCAN HERE
to watch a WILD clip

kyeaqo

Raspy Cricket

Family Gryllacrididae

'Silk-producing insects with ears on their legs.'

What's in a name?

Raspy crickets belong to the order of insects known as the **Orthopterans**. If you love insects as much as I do, you may be familiar with this word, but what does it mean? Orthoptera is derived from the Greek *ortho* meaning 'straight' and *ptera* meaning 'wing'.

Wow, that actually makes a lot of sense when you observe the wings of a raspy cricket.

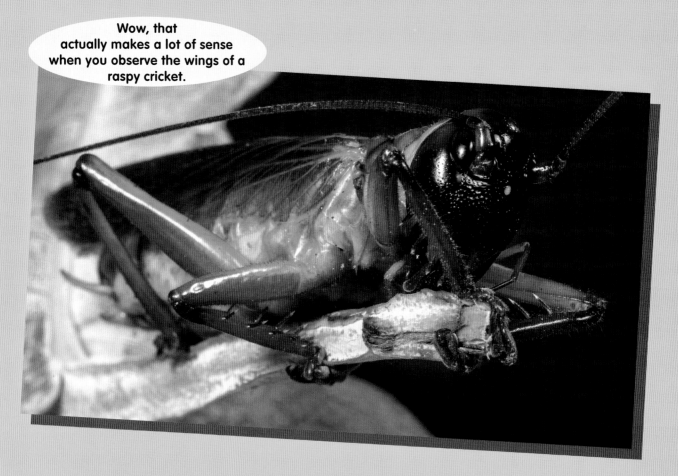

Where are they found?

Raspy crickets are found mostly in the Southern Hemisphere, and amazingly our great country of Australia is blessed with the greatest number of species with more than 120 different types – that's more than one third of all the world's raspy crickets.

In Australia they live in a whole manner of different habitats, including deserts, woodlands, grasslands and even rainforests.

Like many Orthopterans, raspy crickets are extremely important **bioindicators**, reflecting the health and quality of the environments in which they live.

Just like their namesake, these very grumpy insects can make a lot of noise if disturbed or annoyed. They achieve this 'raspy' sound by inflating their abdomen and then rubbing tiny abdominal pegs against tiny spikes on their legs. In science we call this behaviour **femoral-abdominal stridulation**, simply meaning they rub their leg and abdomen together.

Rainforests are among the many habitats that are home to raspy crickets.

Classification

KINGDOM: Animalia
PHYLUM: Arthropoda
CLASS: Insecta
ORDER: Orthoptera
FAMILY: Gryllacrididae

Contrary to popular belief, no insect makes a noise by rubbing its back legs together.

It looks like a giant pair of TV antennae to sense its environment.

Raspy cricket antennae are often longer than their body.

Raspy crickets are usually more active at dusk or at night. Perhaps this is a great way to avoid predation from diurnal birds, reptiles and small mammals?

If you have one of these beasties living in your 'neck of the woods' you live in a biodiverse and healthy place.

Sounds tricky, doesn't it? Raspy crickets also have longer and stockier bodies, and their legs are perpendicular with their bodies, whereas katydid legs are aligned.

Amazing morphology and adaptations

Raspy crickets are closely related to stick insects, grasshoppers, cockroaches and katydids. However, they are unique because they produce silk.

Like all insects, they have three pairs of legs with six segments. However, it's the end of their feet which sets them apart from others. They have three **tarsomeres** (the fancy word for subsegments of the end leg segment!), whereas katydids have four.

Raspy crickets have intricately designed and specialist feet for climbing.

A species of katydid.

Raspy crickets have special 'ears' on their forelegs called **tympana**. It is thought that females listen for the male's serenading love song.

The back legs are specially adapted for jumping. These are called **saltatorial legs** as they are generally longer and larger. Their legs assist them for climbing, jumping and fossicking for their food.

Raspy crickets often travel great distances from their daytime 'hidey-hole' or lair. It is thought that they lay down a pheromonal trail to assist and guide them back to their home.

Hey, that beats using a Sat Nav or Google Maps when you are trying to get somewhere – LOL!

Close up they look like they are wearing an expensive pair of Nike Air shoes.

Raspy crickets have a specialised adaptation of masterfully glueing leaf sheaths together with silk, which they amazingly produce from their mouth parts. They cleverly shelter in their silken leaf tent during the day, to avoid the desiccating sun and predators.

It's a bit like a daytime hammock... so they can have a siesta.

Raspy crickets forage at night for nectar, fruit and small insects. There is a lot more to be learnt and studied about raspy crickets. In fact, many raspy crickets in Australia are yet to be scientifically described.

Although, not considered dangerous to people, raspy crickets 'pack a wallop' when they bite you. They are equipped with sizeable mandibles with sharp incisors, capable of cutting through the skin and giving you an awfully painful bite, even drawing blood!

I would think twice about messing with a raspy cricket once one of these guys latches on to you. I can tell you definitely from personal experience. OUCH!

There is still so much to learn, and there is so much diversity in raspy cricket species – some are believed to be omnivorous, a few herbivorous, and others even carnivorous.

Hey, perhaps you might like to be an entomologist when you are older? You may even discover a new species.

Life Cycle

It is thought that raspy crickets communicate with each other by drumming their legs on their thorax and also drumming the ground. They are believed to do this in courtship to attract a mate.

Once mated, the female deposits her eggs into moist sand or soil with her **ovipositor.**

An ovipositor is a tube-like organ, used to deposit eggs in any damp substrate which is available.

Raspy crickets have three stages in their life cycle: the egg, nymph and adult. After mating a fertile female will lay her eggs, which take about fourteen days to hatch. The nymph is essentially a small version of the adult, however they are not as physically developed, lacking wings and the females do not have ovipositors.

Baby raspy crickets are easy prey for many predators, even larger crickets! As soon as they hatch, a nymph will build a nest or a burrow to conceal themselves.

In order to grow, the nymph raspy cricket sheds its hard exoskeleton. The moulting of the cricket is called **ecdysis** and happens eight to ten times before reaching adulthood.

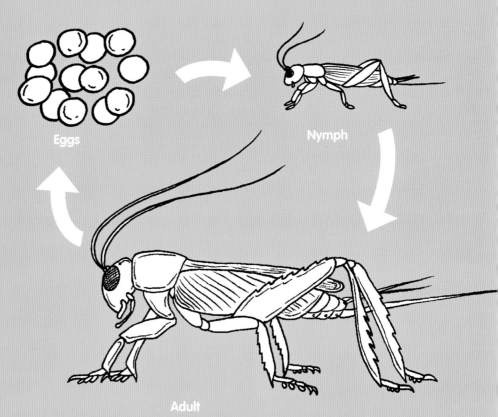

Eggs

Nymph

Adult

Predators and threats

Although many species are well equipped with sharp powerful jaws, raspy crickets are no match for a hungry predator such as a dragon or monitor lizard. Many birds and small mammals would see them as a tasty nutritious snack.

Reptiles, such as a Boyd's Forest Dragon, prey on raspy crickets.

How can we help raspy crickets?

Raspy crickets are thought to be pollinators of many flowering plant species, and are extremely important in ecosystem food webs as they are prey for many animals. They also tell us that we live in a healthy environment, as they are highly susceptible to pollution and nitrogen-rich environments.

You can help raspy crickets by planting native habitat in your back yard or school ground. Avoid using pesticides and herbicides and enjoy sharing the natural world with these amazing yet mysterious orthopterans.

SCAN HERE
to watch a WILD clip

holwww

Snail

Family Caryodidae

'Snails are sometimes considered a pest, however protecting them is always best!'

You can't argue with that description – that's essentially what a snail is.

What's in a name?

The phylum Mollusca is derived from the Latin word *mollis* meaning 'soft'. These soft-bodied animals belonging to one of the largest phyla in the animal kingdom.

The class Gastropoda is ancient Greek for *gastros* meaning 'stomach' and *podos* meaning 'foot'.

Classification

KINGDOM: Animalia
PHYLUM: Mollusca
CLASS: Gastropoda
FAMILY: Caryodidae

Snails belong to the class Gastropoda. This vast group of species consists of slugs and snails from saltwater and freshwater aquatic environments and even from terrestrial environments.

Some species of snail may be considered a pest, and dreaded by gardeners, but just imagine them getting squashed and poisoned in gardens all over Australia every night.

The introduced Garden Snail, despite its 'pest' status, is really a very curious creature indeed, and one often misunderstood and overlooked.

When you look at them close-up, they really are very cute.

For many of us slugs and snails have a very bad reputation. They don't really deserve all of their adverse publicity, because when you study them up close they are very fascinating beasties.

Where are they found?

Snail species are not just confined to people's backyards and veggie patches – they can be found in a wide variety of different habitats and environments, even arid deserts. However, most native land snails are terrestrial and live on the forest floor in amongst moist rotting logs, vegetation and tree debris.

Snails feed on fungus, leaf litter and vegetable matter, although some species are primarily carnivorous.

They are one of the few higher animals which has the capability of breaking down cellulose, which is what plant cell walls are made of.

Unlike their saltwater cousins who typically have gills, land snails and slugs breathe air through a modified mantle chamber which acts as a lung.

WOW, you see they are fantastic detritivores, breaking down organic waste... they really are like garbage collectors.

Amazing morphology and adaptations

A snail is divided into two main parts: the hard shell and soft body. The visceral hump contains the main internal organs and is covered by a thick layer of skin called the **mantle**.

Secreted from glands just under the head, a snail's movement is assisted by a trail of thick mucus which assists them to slide across surfaces, lubricating the path.

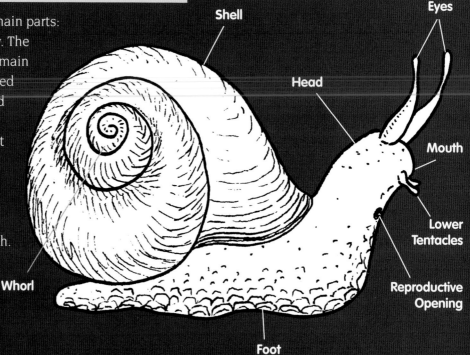

Shell

Eyes

Head

Mouth

Lower Tentacles

Whorl

Reproductive Opening

Foot

That's like a super-long 'slip and slide'.

The mucous dries, leaving behind a snail trail, which the snail uses as a footpath to navigate back to feeding areas, and back to resting sites.

Snails don't have conventional teeth for chewing; however, they do have a highly effective raspy mouth part called the **radula**. This 'scraping' apparatus is covered in horny 'teeth' which are used to rasp away at their food. These horny plates wear out quickly and are continuously replaced from behind as the radula grows forward.

Who would have thought that the humble Garden Snail has something in common with the Great

The blood of snails is practically colourless. Blood carries oxygen throughout the body, also serving as a hydrostatic skeleton.

Snails have two pairs of eye stalks or tentacles, with eyes on the tip of each.

WOW, they are like an in-built periscope on a submarine.

Although snails have poor eyesight, their tentacles can still detect brightness, and allows smell and touch.
Snails have the extraordinary ability to change their blood pressure by muscular contraction. This allows them to change their body shape rapidly and have their tentacles turned inside out.

Amazing! Just Like a balloon filled with water.

Some snails have the ability to survive extended periods of drought by 'battening down the hatches' and retreating into the shell, closing the shell's operculum and sealing it with a hardened mucus membrane preventing moisture loss and desiccation.

They may not be the Ferraris of the mollusc world, but they certainly are great contortionists.

The cool thing about snails is that they are mostly **hermaphrodites**, which means that individuals have both the male and female reproductive organs.

Self-fertilization can occur, however pairing of snails happens more often. Funnily enough, snails choreograph very elaborate, often 'drawn-out' courtship dances, circling each other, foaming and twisting and turning their tentacles about.

The common Garden Snail uses this strategy to reproduce, approaching a potential suitor with the reproductive opening exposed – this is when they release the 'Cupid's dart'.

The dart most probably stimulates the snails to mate and exchange reproductive cells, which are required to fertilize both snails' eggs.

After mating is completed, eggs are laid shortly afterwards in a dark moist location.

Baby snails hatch from their egg looking like miniature adults, however their shell is soft, making them highly susceptible to predation by a myriad of species.

It sounds like a mollusc's version of *The Nutcracker*.

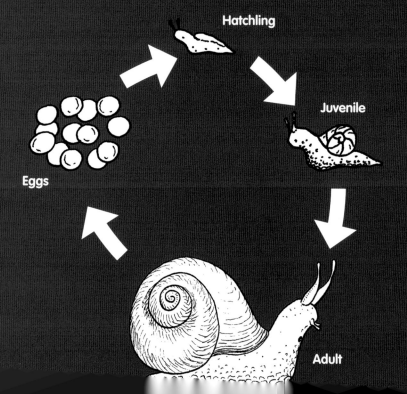

Hatchling

Juvenile

Eggs

Adult

I think that this is the wildest, most amazing thing I have ever heard!

Some species of lizards, such as this Blotched Blue-tongue, are keen predators of snails.

Threats and Predators

Their close association with moisture makes this group of animals extremely important environmental indicators. Many native Australian snail species are threatened by habitat loss, climate change, pesticides and pollution.

Many reptiles and birds relish a feast of snails.

Avoid using dangerous snail baits in your garden or veggie patch, as poisoned snails will end up in the food chain and harm other creatures as well.

What can we do to help snails?

We all need to be a little more sympathetic to snails. Next time you see a snail, don't squash it or poison it. I implore you to stop and marvel at such an amazing animal – one which is an ultimate survivor and deserves our respect!

SCAN HERE
to watch a WILD clip

mkfmme

Emperor Gum Moth

Opodiphthera eucalypti

'Oh, what big eyes you have... all the better to scare you with.'

What's in a name?

The Emperor Gum Moth belongs to the genus *Opodiphthera*, which is **endemic** to Australia – that means it can be found nowhere else on Earth.

Moths and butterflies belong to the order Lepidoptera, which refers to the tiny scales covering their wings. This word is derived from the Ancient Greek words **Lepis** meaning 'scale' and **pteron** meaning 'wing'.

The species name **eucalypti** is a dead giveaway regarding where you may find this beautiful species.

Distribution and habitat

This easily-to-identify nocturnal moth is commonly found around streetlights of eastern Australian towns and cities at night. The natural habitat of the Emperor Gum Moth is eucalyptus forests and woodlands, mainly up the east coast of Australia. It can be found in the Northern Territory, Queensland, New South Wales and Victoria. Surprisingly it was introduced to New Zealand!

As the name suggests, the hungry larval stage caterpillar prefers to feed on eucalyptus leaves, however they have also been recorded feeding on grapevines, silver birch and peppercorn trees.

Classification

KINGDOM:	Animalia
PHYLUM:	Arthropoda
CLASS:	Insecta
ORDER:	Lepidoptera
FAMILY:	Saturniidae
GENUS:	*Opodiphthera*
SPECIES:	*eucalypti*

Amazing morphology and adaptations

The wings of Emperor Gum Moths are covered with minute overlapping **scales**. These scales provide insulation against heat loss. Some moth species can have up to six hundred scales per square millimetre of their wing.

Emperor Gum Moths have wonderfully recognisable big **eye-shaped patterns** on their wings. Perhaps they are adapted to intimidate hungry predators, or possibly target the attention of a predator away from vital more sensitive parts of the body. This would give the moth a better chance of survival if attacked?

It's like wearing a thermal suit.

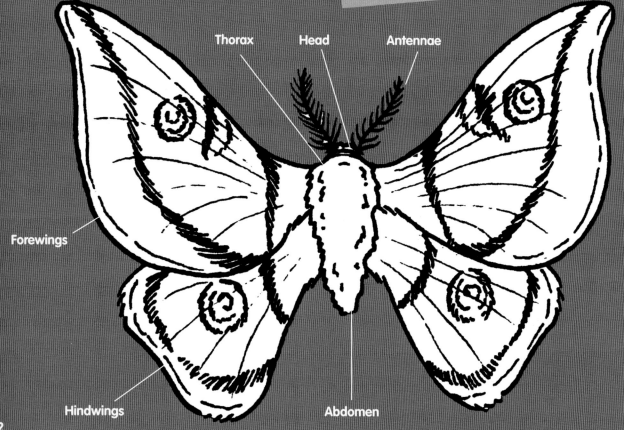

Thorax   Head   Antennae

Forewings

Hindwings   Abdomen

Emperor Gum Moths don't have noses like we do, however they can still 'smell' using **chemoreception**, detecting cues in the environment using sensitive receptors on their antennae. Male moths use chemoreception to 'smell' and are equipped with feathery antennae – the large surface area detects molecules in the air. The females use sex-attractant pheromones to invite potential mates to party!

Male moths have larger antennae than the females for detecting pheromones released by females.

Wow, clever – that actually makes a lot of sense.

The caterpillar of the Emperor Gum Moth has false legs know as **prolegs**. They are perfectly designed for climbing amongst the canopy in their arboreal world. They lose these extra appendages when they metamorphose into a moth.

Did you know that moths, just like their cousins the butterflies, have a special organ at the base of their antenna, used for navigational tasks!

The Johnston's Organ helps the moth to orientate itself in flight and helps it to balance.

You can tell a moth from a butterfly by looking at its antennae. Moths generally have feathery thread-like antennae, whereas butterfly antennae are shaped like clubs with a knob on the very end.

The male moth uses his long antennae to sense for molecules in the air, picking up the female's pheromones from impressive distances.

Did you know that moths can smell without a nose?

Life Cycle

Adult Emperor Gum Moths do not feed. They only have short lives, living for just a couple of weeks. Their mission is to find a mate, lay eggs and then die.

After mating, the female Emperor Gum Moth glues her fertilised eggs onto a eucalyptus leaf, which caterpillars will eat when they emerge. The caterpillars will literally eat their way out of their egg and immediately commence eating gum leaves. The caterpillars are covered in bright **protective spines** to ward off potential predators. The larval caterpillars go through five instars of growth before they build a cocoon and pupate. Surprisingly the spines are harmless!

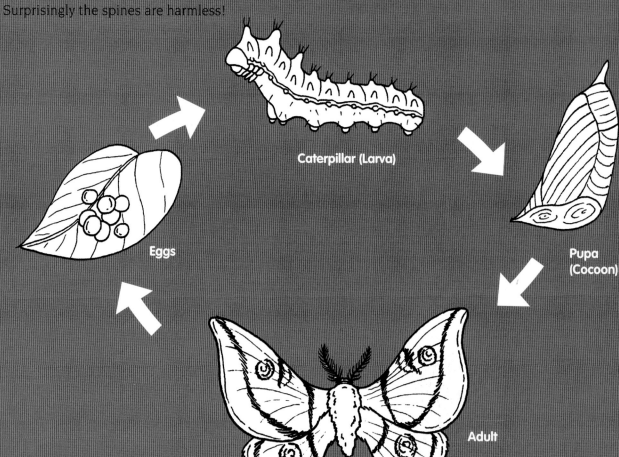

Caterpillar (Larva)

Eggs

Pupa (Cocoon)

Adult

Hey, it looks like Joseph's technicolour dream coat, and it sure looks dangerous.

The pupa remains enclosed in a brown silken cocoon, usually emerging as an adult the following summer. Unfavourable environmental conditions could slow this development for up to five years! The adult moth's forewing is equipped with a distal hook, making light work of ripping out of the cocoon. The soft pink-fawn adult emerges, equipped with feather-duster antennae.

Predators and threats

Despite their warning colours as a caterpillar, and the intimidating 'eyed' wings of the adult, Emperor Gum Moths have many predators. Birds and microbats would relish them as a juicy protein-rich meal.

Emperor Gum Moth populations have noticeably declined in places where they were once common. Loss of suitable habitat, pollution and the invasive European Wasp predating on larvae could all have a negative effect on this beautiful species.

Ghost bats take adult moths in flight.

> **Why not plant native vegetation which Emperor Gum Moth larvae will feed on?**

What can we do to help Emperor Gum Moths?

Like most moth species, Emperor Gum Moths are important pollinators in eucalyptus woodlands and a vital food source for many species of animals.

You can help Emperor Gum Moths by not using insecticides in your garden or on your property.

Mix over-ripe bananas and their skin, molasses and stale beer and paint liberally onto where you want to attract moths.

SCAN HERE
to watch a WILD clip

tsgkhy

If you would like to observe which moth species live in your back yard, why not mix up a fermenting 'moth milkshake', which they can't resist. Smear it over some trees and buildings and wait to see who flutters into your back yard.

Monteith's Leaf Insect

Phyllium monteithi

'Dancing leaf insects – now you see me, now you don't.'

What's in a name?

The genus P*hyllium* contains species of 'true leaf insects' or 'walking leaves'. They are a large and widespread phasmid, found throughout tropical South-East Asia and north-eastern Queensland.

Phasmid (pronounced ***fas***-mid) is derived from ancient Greek meaning 'ghost' or 'phantom', in reference to their amazing camouflage.

The species name ***monteithi*** refers to Queensland scientist **Dr Geoff Monteith** who discovered this amazing beastie.

Classification

KINGDOM:	Animalia
PHYLUM:	Arthropoda
CLASS:	Insecta
ORDER:	Phasmatodea
FAMILY:	Phylliidae
GENUS:	*Phyllium*
SPECIES:	*monteithi*

Where is it found?

Monteith's Leaf Insect has only been recorded from a few locations in warm tropical rainforests in northern Queensland. Because these bugs have truly exceptional camouflage they are rarely seen in the wild. In fact, only two known female specimens have ever been recorded.

Aerial view of rainforest in north Queensland.

They are possibly more common than we think, however finding a wild *Phyllium* is like looking for a needle in a haystack.

The last female was found after Cyclone Ita in 2014, in the Far North Queensland town of Kuranda.

The Monteith's Leaf Insect leads an arboreal lifestyle living high up in the rainforest canopy, avoiding detection from hungry predators. The male can fly and has been known to fly into suburban backyards, attracted to lights in people's dwellings. Herbivorous in nature, this cryptic phasmid dines on the leaves of various rainforest plants.

In captivity they can be difficult to keep. Phyllium leaf insects are very fussy eaters and relish feasting on species of lilly pilly.

Amazing morphology and adaptations

Leaf insects have superb **camouflage** to blend in with the rainforest canopy. Even their wings are adorned with patterns to mimic the veins of a leaf.

They are often referred to as 'dancing' leaf insects. They will rock back and forth like a leaf in the wind. This peculiar behaviour enhances their already super-hero camouflage, enabling them to blend in with the waving leaves in the breeze.

Phasmids have specialised foot pads and hooked feet to help them to climb.

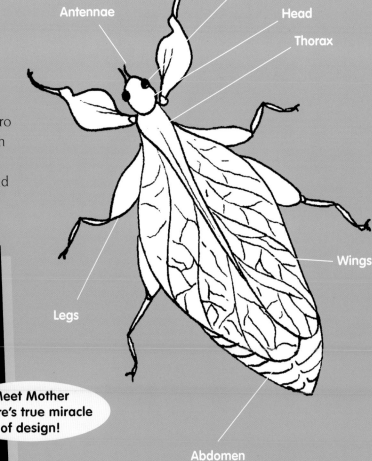

Antennae · Eye · Head · Thorax · Wings · Legs · Abdomen

Meet Mother Nature's true miracle of design!

Monteith's Leaf Insects have compound eyes, as well as ocelli in the middle of their head. The ocelli in this species are filled with photoreceptors and perhaps help them to navigate whilst flying around in their 'high-rise' environment.

A leaf insect's **antennae** help them to 'feel' around the rainforest canopy, and perhaps help them to sense for food and the pheromones of a potential mate.

Spiderman eat your heart out!

Life Cycle

Just like stick insects, leaf insects have an incomplete metamorphosis. The life cycle is only three stages: egg, nymph and adult.

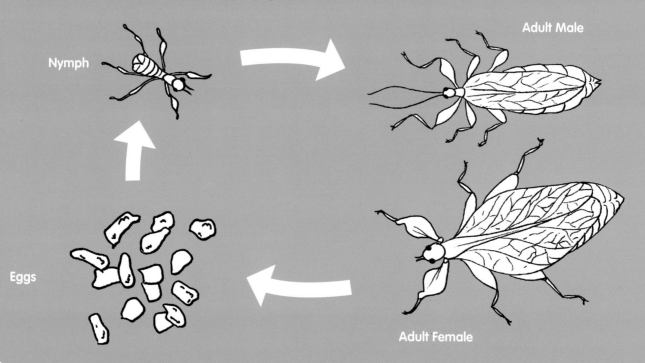

Leaf insects have exoskeletons. As they grow, they need to shed their skin!

> **Hey, that's much cheaper than going to the shops to buy new threads.**

The process of moulting is called **ecdysis** and the stage between successive moults is called an **instar**.

As Monteith's Leaf Insects grow and mature, they become distinguishably **gender dimorphic**.

> **Which means that there are observable differences in body shape between the male and the female.**

The male can be distinguished by his accentuated long antennae and much more noticeable 'lengthy' wings. The female is usually larger, with a much rounder abdomen, with shorter broader wings which lay flat on her back. Females lack under wings and are unable to fly.

Adults will mate and breed all year round. The female will lay her eggs and throw them to the forest floor. The eggs will take four to five months to hatch. Baby leaf insects are called **nymphs**, and are black when they hatch, affording great camouflage. However, as they commence eating, and after their first moult, they turn green to blend in with their arboreal world in the rainforest canopy. The skin that has been shed is full of protein and is eaten by the developing nymph.

> **Oh well, waste not want not in the animal kingdom.**

Incredibly, just like in many phasmids, females can reproduce alone by **parthenogenesis**. When this happens the nymphs are genetic clones of the female.

The Monteith's Leaf Insect will live for up to 15 months.

Predators and Threats

Although *Phyllium* would rarely be encountered by a would-be predator, without defence they could become an easy snack for a hungry bird, amphibian, reptile or even a small mammal.

The wet tropical rainforests of north Queensland face many perils. Habitat destruction and climate change are very real threats to the future survival of the Monteith's Leaf Insect.

What's their job?

Monteith's Leaf Insects are specialised **folivores**, or leaf eaters. They help promote vigour and growth in rainforest trees by eating the leaves

Of course, insects play a vital role in food webs, and form a valuable nutritional addition to the diet of many animal species.

Lesser Sooty Owls feed on leaf insects.

Every animal has a job to do, and leaf insects are no different.

Even in captivity it's hard to see them.

What can we do to help Monteith's Leaf Insects?

Why not create some habitat? Avoid using pesticides and herbicides, and be a responsible pet owner! Although rarely encountered in the wild, Monteith's Leaf Insects are now reasonably common in zoological institutes and the hobby trade. Perhaps you would like to learn more about this intriguing insect by keeping one as a pet and studying its interesting life cycle at home?

Hey, why not help out insects and all sorts of other invertebrates in your school yard or own back yard?

SCAN HERE
to watch a WILD clip

koowvu

Index

First published in 2022 by Reed New Holland Publishers
Sydney

Level 1, 178 Fox Valley Road, Wahroonga, NSW 2076, Australia

newhollandpublishers.com

A record of this book is held at the National Library of Australia.

ISBN 978 1 76079 445 3

Managing Director: Fiona Schultz
Publisher and Project Editor: Simon Papps
Designer: Andrew Davies
Production Director: Arlene Gippert

Printed in China

10 9 8 7 6 5 4 3 2 1

Also available from Reed New Holland:

Chris Humfrey's Awesome Australian Animals
ISBN 978 1 92554 670 5

Colour With Chris Humfrey's Awesome Australian Animals
ISBN 978 1 76079 424 8

For details of hundreds of other Natural History titles see newhollandpublishers.com

And keep up with New Holland Publishers:

 NewHollandPublishers and ReedNewHolland

 @newhollandpublishers

RHINOCEROS BEE

SPECTRE STICK I

WORM 22 GARDEN

RAINFOREST MAN

48 CENTIPEDE

TARANTULA 62

SCORPION 70 BU

WATER YABBY 8

94 SNAIL 102 EM

110 MONTEITH'S